"I loved this book! . . . I highly recommend it."

"I loved this book! It was a real eye-opener. As a teacher, I have always known there was a link between behavior, nutrition, and student learning, but I didn't have anything to back up my suspicions. Also, when a perfect angel in the morning was a terror in the afternoon, I often attributed it to tiredness. This book helped me understand what else is going on in those little bodies. This book is a wonderful resource for teachers and parents. I highly recommend it."

Tresa Cummins
National Board-Certified Teacher
Norwood, North Carolina

"This idea works."

"*Bad Attitude* teaches us that food is one of the main culprits behind our kids' behavior and their health. Congratulations—this is one message that desperately needs to get out. Take it from me, this idea works."

Fred Pescatore, M.D.
Author of *Feed Your Kids Well* and *Thin for Good*

". . . Wonderful . . . Especially helpful are the specific menus and recipes."

"Doctors Ricker and Cabin have put together a wonderful manual on dealing with rudeness in children. While the focus is on how food choices can have a major impact on bad attitude, they also deal with other important topics such as food allergies, eating disorders, and good health habits such as hydration, sleep, and exercise. Especially helpful are the specific menus and recipes they include for those of us who need to be taken by the hand.

My children are a bit older now, but my sense is that this approach would also make a big difference with them or, for that matter, with anyone at any age."

Richard Ruiz, Ph.D.
International Consultant, Education and Language
Professor, College of Education
University of Arizona

"Positive steps for changing bad attitudes"

"I appreciate how this book identifies rude behaviors, encourages people not to accept such behaviors, and suggests positive steps for changing bad attitudes that are caused by poor nutrition. It lets parents, grandparents, teachers, and others know, through clearly presented facts, how food "treats" may be causing physiological and attitude problems in children. I especially liked the message that you can show how much you really love your children by being firm in providing them with healthful meals and ending their use of junk food.

I also like how this book presents both a solid rationale for modifying eating habits and gives specific, practical steps for putting food reform into action in your home."

William J. Valmont, Ph.D.
Director of Technology and Professor
of Language, Reading, and Culture
University of Arizona

"Delightful . . . Practical . . . Puts parents firmly in charge."

"Parents, grandparents, and teachers will love this delightful book. It's easy to read and understand and loaded with helpful information. Its basic message: What a child takes into his stomach plays a key role in how he behaves.

The book provides parents with practical tips and menu plans, including advice for holidays. By following it, parents will not only be able to provide their children with proper nutrition, but they will also put themselves firmly in charge of the household."

William G. Crook, M.D.
Emeritus Fellow, American Academy of Pediatrics
Author of *The Yeast Connection Handbook*

"An absolute must. . . . I will recommend it to all my patients."

"The authors have provided unbiased, easy to understand, essential nutritional information for any parent, but an absolute must for parents of difficult children. I will recommend it to all my patients."

Bruce Roseman, M.D.
Author of *A Kid Just Like Me:*
A Father and Son Overcome the Challenges
of ADD and Learning Disabilities

"Every parent, teacher, and policy maker must take notice. We ignore the message of this book at our peril."

"As a social scientist, researcher, and ethicist, it took me too long to come to the deep understanding that is the message of this book—the nutrients and electricity in our brain cells are responsible for our behavior. Healthy humans require a healthy balance of these components. Lacking such awareness, we continue to poison our children and ourselves and experience dramatically devastating results. Every parent, teacher, and policy maker must take notice. We ignore the message of this book at our peril."

Ann Noe Dapice, Ph.D.
Educator and Nutrition Counselor
Tulsa, Oklahoma

"Dr. Ricker's recommendations are first class."

"Again, Dr. Ricker has written a book that anyone can enjoy and use. The examples are extremely appropriate in demonstrating how children's physiological and emotional fluctuations are affected by the foods they consume throughout the day. The suggestions and recommendations Dr. Ricker makes for altering children's nutritional intake to control mood swings and health are first class."

Taralynn Hartsell, Ph.D.
Assistant Professor of Instructional Design
College of Technology Education
University of Southern Mississippi

"Recipes that put a child and family back on the right track."

"Parents of young children who are struggling with difficult behavior *must* read this book. It provides documented, concrete, and "do-able" suggestions that will fit easily in any family's lifestyle. This book provides insight into an often overlooked area of need for many children and literally provides recipes that put a child and family back on the right track."

Joanne Knapp-Philo, Ph.D.
SpecialQuest Director
Hilton/Early Head Start Training Program
California Institute on Human Services

BAD attitude

Reverse Your Child's Rudeness in 1 Week—*With Food*

FROM THE AUTHOR OF *BACKTALK*

Audrey Ricker, Ph.D.

WITH BRIAN CABIN, M.D., M.D.(H).

RODALE

Notice

This book is intended as a reference volume only, not as a medical manual. The information given here is designed to help you make informed decisions about your child's health. It is not intended as a substitute for any treatment that may have been prescribed by your child's doctor. If you suspect that your child has a medical problem, we urge you to seek competent medical help.

Mention of specific companies, organizations, or authorities in this book does not imply endorsement by the publisher, nor does mention of specific companies, organizations, or authorities imply that they endorse the book.

Internet addresses and telephone numbers given in this book were accurate at the time it went to press.

Printed in the United States of America
Rodale Inc. makes every effort to use acid-free ∞, recycled paper ♻.
Interior and cover design by Tara Long

Library of Congress Cataloging-in-Publication Data

Ricker, Audrey.
    Bad attitude : reverse your child's rudeness in 1 week—with food /
from the author of Backtalk, Audrey Ricker, with Brian Cabin.
        p.   cm.
    Includes bibliographical references and index.
    ISBN 1–57954–590–4 paperback
    1. Aggressiveness in children—Nutritional aspects.   I. Cabin,
Brian. II. Title.
[DNLM: 1. Child Behavior—Popular Works. 2. Diet—adverse
effects—Child—Popular Works. 3. Child Nutrition—Popular Works.
4. Child Rearing—Popular Works. WS 130 R539b 2002]
RJ506.A35 R53 2002
649'.4—dc21   2002003449

Distributed to the book trade by St. Martin's Press

2 4 6 8 10 9 7 5 3 1   paperback

To Lynn Wiese-Sneyd,
for her generous, wise, and constantly
available friendship and support.
—Audrey Ricker

To my fiancée,
Mary Elizabeth Aivazian,
for her encouragement, tireless
support, love, and friendship.
—Brian Cabin

contents

acknowledgments

I want to thank Robert E. Calmes, Ed.D., for so generously sharing his six-step plan. I also want to thank my agent, Vince Desiderio. I want to acknowledge Lou Cinquino and Amy Kovalski for their careful, creative editing and Lori Davis for her invaluable research. Finally, I am eager to thank Brian Cabin, M.D., M.D.(H)., for his open-mindedness about medical issues dealing with children's well-being.

—*Audrey Ricker*

I want to thank my classmate and good friend Edwin Funk, M.D., for introducing me to homeopathy and natural medicine throughout medical school; my mother, Dorothy Cabin, who inspired learning and whose ravenous reading and intellectual curiosity included nutrition and natural medicine; and my aunts, Dinah Polen and Elaine Esch, for bravely pursuing drug-free medical care when they were the only people I knew who did so. I want to acknowledge Dr. Robert Fulford, the late, great osteopath and homeopath who spent hours teaching me to feel and think outside the box.

Thanks especially to all of my wonderful patients, who have been my truest teachers. I love practicing medicine, and it is truly an honor to serve you.

And to the readers who are opening their hearts and minds to living a healthier and fuller life, I salute you.

—*Brian Cabin*

introduction

There's one very simple reason behind my passionate determination to write the book you are reading now:

The discipline methods in my previous books didn't always work.

As coauthor of two other books on children's behavior, *Backtalk: Four Steps to Ending Rude Behavior in Your Kids* and *Whining: Three Steps to Stopping It Before the Tears and Tantrums Start*, I thought I had a handle on stopping rudeness in kids. The advice in these books is based on psychological principles and literally tends to work like magic. When a child is rude, whiny, or displays other unwanted behavior, the parent enacts a consequence that the child dislikes. The child will, in order to avoid facing the consequence again, stop that behavior. Many, many readers told me that this simple idea had changed their lives for the better, put them in charge of their homes again, and made their children treat them with respect. (I'll provide a new version of methods like these in chapter 7 of this book so you can try them yourself.)

But I began hearing from some parents who did everything these books advised and still were unable to stop their children's rudeness. "The strategies you recommend in your book are useless with my child," one mom said. "I've taken all kinds of privileges away from my son as consequences for his backtalk, and still he is terrible to me. Frankly, I've run out of any new consequences to use!" Other parents said the consequences they imposed stopped their children's rudeness for a few hours, but no longer. Still others reported that the consequences had stopped the backtalk for a week or so, and they had thought the problem was solved. But soon, the rudeness would begin again, causing the parents to feel as though nothing had been accomplished. My coauthor, a trained Adlerian psychologist, attributed these failures to parental "misapplication" of the advice in our books. There may have been some truth to that, but I knew the answer was just not that simple. These parents deserved a better answer than that.

Clearly, some kids' rudeness was beyond the control of any ultimatum, consequence, or other behavioral strategy. What on Earth, I agonized, was going on with these kids who couldn't be helped by the strategies that had worked so well for others?

A Parent's Intuition

As I was pondering the question of this unexplained rudeness, I thought back to my own experiences raising my son. I recalled that he had been unbearably rude at times—until I noticed that he acted especially awful when he ate anything with sugar in it or drank any sugar-sweetened, artificially colored beverage. That kind of physiological response to foods heavy in sugar or refined carbohydrates ran in my family, so I hadn't been surprised that my son was the same way. I quickly learned to restrict the amount of these foods in his diet—something that significantly improved his be-havior and, I believe, did a lot to help him lead a happy, productive life.

Could diet also be a factor in the rudeness of the children whose parents had written me? I suspected it might. And I was sure that these weren't isolated cases.

A Scientist's Observations

Because I am a scientist as well as a parent, I have had unique op-portunities to observe children's behavior in an objective, detached way. One research study I completed a few years ago seemed par-ticularly intriguing as I pondered causes of rudeness in children. This project required me to spend more than 120 hours in the homes of middle school students, observing their use of television, video games, and other media between the time they got home from school and when their parents arrived home from work. The most interesting observation I made during this study, though, concerned the children's diets rather than their media use.

I noticed that all of the participants were allowed whatever foods they liked, whenever they wanted them. This diet was a far cry from the kind I had grown up on, which was heavy on meat, pota-toes, vegetables, and fruit. As a child, I usually had fruit for my snacks, and I was allowed sweets only for dessert, at birthday par-ties, and during outings to the ice cream store. In stark contrast, the kids in the study seemed to have sugar and grease as their staple foods.

After a half-hour or so of gorging on chips, ice cream, soda, and cake in various combinations (they tended to go from sweet foods—covered with canned whipped cream in one home—to salty snacks, such as chips), these subjects would, I observed, all become sullen and rude. Their attitudes toward me would go from being positive and productive, as in, "Hi, Audrey! Come see the algebra homework program I just got!" to negative and counterproductive. ("I don't want to do the algebra program. I think I hate that program. Isn't it time for you to go home?") They would begin calling one another obscenities and would get into fights. Their energy levels would roller-coaster from hyper-high to a sluggish low—resulting in deep sleep or restless attempts to start activities, such as doing homework or playing some basketball, that soon ran out of steam. I saw these dramatic, dysfunctional swings in attitude and behavior happen like clockwork nearly every day of my study.

The pieces of this puzzle were beginning to assemble into a clear picture: A poor diet—one high in processed snacks, sugary treats, and fast food—must play a role in otherwise unexplainable rude and aggressive behavior in children. This was something I had intuitively known as a parent and seen time and time again as an objective observer in research studies. Yet as I delved deeper into the occurrences of diet-related behavior changes, I soon came to realize that the extent of this problem might be larger than I had ever imagined.

Teachers and Parents Report Increased Rudeness in Kids

About this time, I participated in a study of more than 50 teachers in six states. My job was to ask them, in group interviews, what emotional and physical changes they had seen in students in the past 6 years.

Increases in rude, out-of-control behavior and in bad attitudes in class were the most startling changes noted by all the teachers I interviewed. It didn't matter what discipline methods these teachers used, the students' rudeness would be uncontrollable—especially after lunch. True, this behavior didn't apply to every student and didn't happen every day, but it was now happening often enough, these teachers said, to make their jobs a lot more difficult.

Next, I began questioning parents of children of all ages. Yes, most of them said, their kids' bad attitudes *had* gotten worse in the past few years. These parents most often reported uncontrolled outbursts, negative thinking, and hateful words. It is as though, one parent put it, "a demon possesses them from time to time."

Media Reports of Rudeness on the Rise

I also noticed a disturbing rise in the number of news accounts reporting acts of aggressive, antisocial behavior by children. I'm not talking about acts of violence such as schoolyard killings. Such incidents of children acting out are beyond the scope of this book and the solutions offered. I'm talking about bullying, verbal threats, making false reports to authorities about parental or teacher abuse, and other bad-attitude behaviors children didn't seem to display 30, 20, even 10 years ago. Children in these news stories tended to be from functional families in good communities. Yet something was clearly wrong.

Medical Evidence for My Suspicions

My next step was to pore over research I had done for a book on nutrition, *Smart Guide to Healing Supplements*. My research showed that there was basic medical evidence proving that certain foods and ingredients—such as caffeine and sugar—could affect mood and energy levels. But my studies also revealed a gaping hole in the amount of research done in this field. Though parents have suspected a link between certain foods and poor behavior for years—even decades—science simply hasn't caught up. And though additional studies are currently under way, the scientific method is slow and laborious, and conclusively proving such a link could take years. Clearly, the children who suffer from uncontrollable rudeness (and the parents who love them) can't wait that long for an answer.

It was then that my goal became clear: I would gather the information on what currently *is* known in medical circles about diet-related behavioral changes. I would then add to that information the anecdotal evidence that parents, teachers, and other child-care providers have observed for decades. For the first time, parents wouldn't have to rely on intuition and trial and error when they observed what they suspected to be diet-caused behavioral problems. Best of all, this resource would include all the best advice available for transforming a rude child's behavior. After all, if a poor diet caused poor behavior, I knew that a healthful diet must support healthy, happy behavior. I recognized that I wasn't the only parent who had employed some common-sense strategies to improve my child's behavior problems, and that if I gathered these strategies along with solid medical and nutritional advice, parents could once again take charge of their children's behavior.

United in a Common Mission

One doctor who has proved invaluable to me and who shares my mission to help parents deal with food-induced rudeness is Brian Cabin, M.D., M.D.(H), a pediatrician, general practitioner, and board-certified homeopathic physician who practices in Tucson and has been dealing with the food-behavior connection in his work for years. He has visiting privileges in two of the most prestigious Tucson hospitals and has been a lecturer and member of Dr. Andrew Weil's integrative medicine department at the University of Arizona College of Medicine.

Dr. Cabin not only provided the scientific explanations for my observations, but said that he believes food-caused poor behavior affects huge numbers of children. Certain foods can indeed make kids feel—and act—bad, Dr. Cabin said, while other kinds of foods can make them feel positive, productive, and peace-loving. "You can change many kids' behavior with diet in about 5 days," Dr. Cabin stated unequivocally. "I think more people involved with child-rearing should realize this fact and use it."

Of course, Dr. Cabin is not the only medical authority who has seen this connection. There are many experts who believe that the way we eat can have a bearing on the way we feel and, thus, on the way we act, and I'll share some of their research with you as well. Further, though diet will affect the emotional health of some children more than others, all children will be affected to some extent.

As you read on, you'll discover:

- How to tell if your child suffers from diet-related behavioral problems
- The physiological conditions that can cause bad attitude and rudeness, how to find out if your child has them, and the nutritional solutions that can ease these symptoms
- The surprising list of best and worst foods for your child's mood and attitude
- "Consequence strategies" of child discipline, and ways to integrate nutritional solutions for optimal results
- How to easily plan your child's menu—and great recipes that she'll love to eat!

- Fun ways to celebrate special occasions without going over-board on sugary treats
- Smart tactics that make it quick and easy for your child to choose the right kinds of foods, even when you're not around
- A proven way to make lasting changes in your family's way of life to ensure a more peaceful and harmonious home

With Your Help, Results in 1 Week

At the core of all of my advice in this book is my belief that your children need your love, help, and support with their food choices. Believe me, children with food-induced rudeness feel as awful as they are making you feel with their antics. They are in real trouble and need you to intervene. Their actions and emotions are beyond their control, and they have no idea why.

By taking the practical advice in this book and applying it with love, you will be helping your kids not only act better, but feel better—physically and emotionally. And don't worry: Even if your children have spent years picking up bad food habits, a few simple changes in what they eat and how they eat it—along with some sound discipline strategies—can bring better attitude and behavior in as little as 1 week.

part 1

How Food Affects Your Child's Body and Behavior

1

is food causing your child's rudeness?

Working as a pediatrician and homeopath for more than 2 decades, Brian Cabin, M.D., M.D.(H) has seen more than his share of irritable, frustrated children. Through the years, he has also met a large number of children for whom sullen, antisocial behavior had become a way of life. Yet they had no previously diagnosed medical condition that could account for this behavior, and their parents had tried everything they could to properly discipline them. Dr. Cabin soon realized that what all of these children had in common were poor diets that were high in processed, sugary foods and low in fresh fruits, vegetables, and fiber. Fortunately, these kids also came to share one other striking similarity: greatly improved moods and attitudes as a result of Dr. Cabin's dietary recommendations. One of the most dramatic changes occurred in a teenage patient I'll call Clark. (For matters of privacy, all names have been changed in the cases included in this book.)

When Clark's parents, Sue and Doug Peterson, first consulted Dr. Cabin, they were in despair over their son's behavior. They thought they had provided everything they could for their children. They had moved to the sunny Sonoran desert from a smog-ridden eastern city so their kids could breathe clean air and enjoy outdoor sports. But by the time Clark reached the age of 13, he was as apathetic, difficult to be around, and uninterested in life as if he had grown up next to a smokestack. Sue and Doug suspected that this was much more than just the onset of puberty, and they hoped Dr. Cabin could help them uncover what was at the root of their son's negative outlook. What a happy, loving child he had once been! And what a tired, disinterested, grumbling teenager he had become, they lamented.

Dr. Cabin asked Sue and Doug detailed questions about their son's eating habits. While he ate a healthful dinner with them at night, Clark refused to eat anything for breakfast. For lunch, he had pizza and/or hot dogs or whatever was served at school, washed down with sugared soda. He also visited the school snack machines several times a day for sweets and chips and more sodas.

Next, Dr. Cabin ran a number of diagnostic tests on Clark. One test showed his blood sugar to be 58 milligrams per deciliter (mg/dl), which is very low, especially considering that, contrary to instructions, Clark had eaten just before blood was drawn for this test. (The normal score for blood sugar after fasting is 70 to 110 mg/dl; 2 hours after sitting down to a meal high in carbohydrates, the normal score is 130 to 180 mg/dl.) In addition, Clark's iron level was low as a result of an iron-deficient diet, which resulted in mild anemia. Dr. Cabin's medical diagnosis of Clark was hypoglycemia resulting from poor diet and stress, along with iron deficiency anemia. He recommended putting Clark on a hypoglycemic diet to help regulate his blood sugar levels. The diet consisted of high-quality unprocessed organic foods.

In addition, Dr. Cabin instructed Clark's parents to give him five small meals a day, including breakfast (which he was now told he had to eat). These meals were to include lean protein and were to be very low in refined carbohydrates. His diet became one of fish, chicken, beans, nuts, seeds, vegetables, fruit, and whole grains. By eating healthful foods every 3 to 4 hours, or "grazing," Clark would find that his blood sugar levels would become more stable, decreasing the likelihood that he would experience the severe mood swings that are a result of dramatic changes in blood sugar levels.

Next, Dr. Cabin recommended that Clark take a number of supplements. He prescribed iron picolinate, which is easily absorbed, as well as multivitamins with chromium. He also suggested that Clark begin taking flaxseed, which is a source of omega-3 fatty acids, "good" fats that may decrease the incidence of depression.

Finally, Dr. Cabin and the Petersons had a sort of "intervention" with Clark during which they told him his life would go from its current unhappy state to much worse if he didn't change his eating habits according to their instructions. They told him they were willing to help him as much as they could, but he would have to give up the sweets, chips, and sodas at school on his own. They were all heartened to hear him say he would do so. Sue began packing Clark's lunches for him on some days; on others, she picked him up and took him to a health food salad and juice bar for lunch. Contrary to his expectations, Clark began to enjoy these lunches with his mother, often inviting other students to join them.

Over the next 3 months, Clark's fatigue diminished. Rather than moping around the house, he became much more interested in

physical activities and began to pursue some extracurricular interests. His mood brightened, and he became more emotionally balanced, making him and the people surrounding him much
happier. Clark and his parents were, and still are, delighted with
these results.

Clark isn't the only child who has experienced a dramatic positive change in his attitude and outlook on life as a result of Dr.
Cabin's nutritional advice. In fact, Dr. Cabin has treated so many
children in his pediatric practice who had similar problems that
he's convinced diet-related behavioral problems are a serious national health concern. Yet he's quick to point out that there is hope
for these troubled children—and their parents.

How can you determine if your child is experiencing behavioral
problems as a result of the foods he eats? First, you'll need to take
a close look at your child's relationship with food, paying particular
attention to his behavior patterns after he eats certain types of food.
To help with this, take the following quiz. Write a "T" for true or
"F" for false before each statement.

_____ 1. My child insists on eating foods that contain
          sugar, such as sweetened breakfast cereals, sodas
          and sweetened fruit juices, and candy and cookies.

_____ 2. Often, my child will eat only food that is white,
          such as rice, bread, potatoes, pasta, biscuits, and
          dough-wrapped side dishes.

_____ 3. My child loves cake icing. She always wants the
          piece of cake with the most icing, and if we make

a cake at home, she ends up eating the icing right from the bowl or can.

_____ 4. Once he gets started, my child will snack for hours.

_____ 5. My child does not seem to enjoy vegetables unless they are on pizza or deep fried.

_____ 6. My child's idea of a normal meal is a fast-food burger, french fries, and a soda or thick milkshake, followed by ice cream, cookies, or cake.

_____ 7. My child would choose a side order of macaroni and cheese over any kind of vegetable like carrots, green beans, or peas.

_____ 8. I notice that my child is rude or unpleasant after eating.

_____ 9. It's really hard to say when my child finishes eating—he's snacking before and after every meal.

_____ 10. My child prefers processed lunchmeat sandwiches on white bread as his favorite lunch.

_____ 11. I sometimes use my child's favorite foods as a reward, treat, bribe, or form of entertainment, as in "If you'll stop whining during the car ride, I'll get you some chocolate chip cookies as soon as we get to the mall."

_____ 12. My child can be unexpectedly rude—out of the blue, he'll just snap at me for no good reason.

_____ 13. My child sometimes gets very sleepy after eating sugary foods.

_____ 14. My child becomes very upset and agitated if I tell him "no" when he asks for candy.

_____ 15. My child complains of stomachaches and sometimes has trouble going to the bathroom due to constipation.

_____ 16. My child acts differently when he has had foods with dyes and additives in them.

_____ 17. At parties or other occasions where he eats a lot of sweets, my child will become confused about the rules of the games played and have trouble paying attention.

_____ 18. Sometimes after eating certain foods, my child starts trembling and actually seems shaky.

_____ 19. After eating sweet foods or drinks, my child becomes clumsy and seems uncoordinated.

_____ 20. There are times when my child honestly believes we don't love him and tells us, loudly, how we neglect and mistreat him. But at other times, he is fine with the kind of parenting he gets from us.

Now count up the number of Ts. More than six means that your child is demonstrating signs of food-induced behavioral changes or could be headed for such a problem.

No matter what you do with discipline or behavior modification, if your child is suffering from a physical reaction to the food he is eating, he simply won't be capable of acting the way you want him to act. Further, food-caused rudeness can be progressive in intensity. The minor symptom you observe today could develop into full-scale rage attacks later on. Parents, teachers, and medical doctors all across the country have observed this food-behavior connection, but there has never been an easy-to-understand way to approach and solve the problem, until now.

Good News

You're to be commended for taking the first step: recognizing that food could be the source of your child's attitude problems. The good news is that you are not alone—and you are not powerless. Later chapters of this book will show you how to incorporate Dr. Cabin's practical nutritional strategies into your child's life. Coupled with the sound parenting advice advocated in these pages, these strategies can produce dramatic positive changes in your child's behavior, often in just a week's time.

As you read, you'll probably be surprised to discover all the little-known ways that food affects behavior. In fact, after speaking with parents, educators, and medical professionals, it's clear to me that there are still a lot of myths surrounding the effects that food can have on children's attitudes and behavior. Because understanding the biological and emotional causes of your child's antisocial behavior is the key to stopping it, let's take some time now to dispel the most common fallacies about diet-induced rudeness.

The Biggest Food Fallacies

Here are the most pervasive fallacies that prevent people from understanding the food-behavior connection. We'll take each one in turn and explore why, according to the experiences of Dr. Cabin and others, each is a myth.

Food fallacy #1: Rudeness is a direct result of poor discipline from parents.

Just as often, rudeness is a result of other factors that even the most discipline-oriented parents fail to see and correct. Rudeness can be the result of a child imitating characters on television shows and video games. It can be learned from your child's peers or friends at school.

But rudeness can also be triggered by certain foods. Even the most carefully brought-up, well-disciplined child can turn rude after eating foods with refined flour and sugar or certain additives. Rudeness can be caused by foods that slow digestion or provide empty calories or stimulants. Rudeness is also a result of diets that actually alter the brain's performance in ways that seem to change the child's personality from happy to horrid, from cooperative to cruel.

If they fail to understand this food-behavior connection, parents risk exacerbating the child's situation with even harsher disciplinary tactics, to no avail. As much as the child may want to cooperate, his body will not.

Food fallacy #2: Emotions are separate from physiology.

If not fueled properly by the right foods, your child's body will experience a drop in "nutrition fuel," which sends distress signals to the brain. The child's brain responds with cravings for more food, as well as with feelings of suspicion and hostility. Such feelings make the child feel miserable and behave in ways that are correctly perceived by unsuspecting loved ones as rude.

Even the most cheerful people aren't as pleasant when they're not feeling well, and your child's developing body is particularly prone to this effect.

Food fallacy #3: Kids don't get constipated. And even if they do, it has nothing to do with their behavior.

Many American kids eat a diet that is high in processed foods and low in fruits, vegetables, and whole grains. Unfortunately, this type of diet provides very little fiber. As a result, food tends to bulk up in the intestinal tract and can cause a chronic state of constipation. Besides the physical discomforts of this condition, constipation can also cause kids to feel emotionally upset. These feelings make the child display rude behaviors best described as discontented, dissatisfied, and disinterested in doing anything anyone—especially parents—might want him to do.

Food fallacy #4: It's always okay to give your child as much fruit as he wants.

True, many experts suggest that at least five servings of fruit a day can help prevent disease. But if the fruits are high in sugar—such as grapes, watermelon, dates, and figs—they can cause the same miserable feelings and rude behaviors in kids that refined sugar and flour produce. Dr. Cabin advises limiting kids to two servings of fruit a day, one of which should be an apple or orange since these fruits contain less sugar and more fiber than other varieties. The other fruits should be varied in type throughout the week.

Food fallacy #5: You don't have to watch your child's calorie or protein intake.

While you don't want to force your kids onto a diet that can lead to unhealthy eating disorders, it does make sense to plan out their menus with an eye toward making sure they get appropriate levels of calories and protein for their age and activity level. (For recommended calorie and protein intakes per age group, see page 74.) This is an early way to fight the growing problem of childhood obesity as well as to ensure that the calories your children are consuming are full of nutrients that will keep their systems in balance.

Proteins are made up of 20 amino acids. Without all 20, a child will not develop properly, mentally or physically. His body will manufacture some of these proteins on its own, but the rest must be supplied from foods, such as animal products, that are considered "complete" protein sources. Soy is the only plant-based food that is a source of complete protein. Vegetables, nuts, and seeds are regarded as "incomplete" proteins because they lack or have limited amounts of one or more of the essential amino acids.

Food fallacy #6: How and when my child drinks water is irrelevant to his behavior.

The nervous system must be kept hydrated in order to function well, and water is the best source of that hydration. A child who doesn't get enough water suffers from bad nerves—literally! He'll be irritable and mean and not know why. But to be effective, the water should be consumed regularly throughout the day. Your child should drink eight 8-ounce glasses of water per day. Also, he should drink an additional glass of water for each caffeinated beverage he consumes, since caffeine depletes the body of fluids.

If, however, a large amount of water is consumed with a meal, it could interfere with the digestive juices and enzymes and prevent food from being broken down and absorbed properly by the body. Ideally, no water (or other liquid) should be drunk an hour before to an hour after meals. If your children find this to be too difficult, allow them to have 4 to 6 ounces of liquid while they eat. "The idea is to avoid allowing kids to guzzle down liquid with their meals," explains Dr. Cabin. "Besides hampering optimum digestion, the liquid interferes with appetite and tasting of the food."

Food fallacy #7: Sugar is the only food that will affect my child's behavior.

Everything your child eats has the potential to affect his behavior in some way, since his body's systems rely on food for fuel power. In addition to sugar, especially troublesome are all foods with high amounts of carbohydrates, especially the simple carbs, which are absorbed quickly by the body. These foods include breads, muffins, sweet and white potatoes, bananas, grapes, sweetened cereals, sodas, cakes, candies, cookies, and pastries. According to Dr. Cabin, these foods can trigger hypoglycemic episodes in some children. We'll discuss this condition in depth in chapter 4, along with other physical conditions that affect behavior.

Foods with dyes in them can also cause rude and uncontrollable behavior by irritating the nervous system. Be wary of icings, cereals, colored ketchups, frozen ice pops, commercial vitamins, and any other food that lists natural or artificial colors in the ingredients list. Foods that contain caffeine are other known culprits of behavioral problems. Some parents report that after their children drink a caffeinated beverage, they act as though they're possessed by demons—sometimes for as long as 48 hours. Some kids are born with the inability to handle these foods; others spontaneously develop this inability at some point in their childhoods. Rudeness then becomes a way of life for these children.

Food fallacy #8: There are no decent substitutes for sugar.

Stevia is a natural, sweet-tasting supplement used to sweeten foods and recommended by Dr. Cabin in his practice. While it has not been approved by the FDA as a sweetener, it has been found to have no more negative side effects than saccharine and aspartame—both of which have been approved by the FDA—and many more nutritive benefits. You'll learn more about stevia, including how to cook with it, later in this book.

Honey and fructose, the sugar found in fruit, are certainly preferable to sucrose (refined white sugar) because they are absorbed by the body less quickly and, particularly in the case of honey, provide some nutritive value. Ultimately, however, they can have the same rudeness-causing effect on the body as refined sugar. (*Note:* Do not give honey to children who are younger than 12 months. It contains dormant spores that are harmless to children and adults but may cause botulism in infants.)

Food fallacy #9: My kids will never go for it.

This is the biggest fallacy of them all. You are your children's best teacher. If you don't teach them how to eat properly, who will? Maybe they won't learn right away, but just like other skills you've taught them, they will learn. And once they do, you'll be helping them stay happy and healthy their entire lives.

Unless you show them the way, most kids will go for the nutritionally unsound foods every time—these goodies are instantly gratifying and in some cases addictive. But kids are not stupid. They can learn which foods will keep them from feeling their best and learn to love the foods that are good for them in the long run.

Still don't believe your children will listen to your advice? Consider that extensive research by the U.S. government on childhood drug abuse has revealed that children who received clear and consistent communication from their parents about drugs were much less likely to develop problems with illicit drugs. You see, children want what their families want for them. But the adults have to tell them what they want, frequently, in positive, affirming ways, and model the behavior they want from the children.

In this book, you'll learn how to help your children choose the most healthful foods. Soon, you'll find them actually preferring the healthful choices. Why? Because once children give them a chance, they discover that these foods are marvelously delicious. Yes, it takes a bit of effort for kids to give up foods that have been processed, sweetened, and greased beyond recognition for foods in their natural, whole form—but once they do, they'll be so turned off by those "ugly" foods, they won't go back.

Food fallacies have kept many American parents from even trying to educate their kids about nutrition—and allowed too many kids to become frustrated and act rudely in ways that may now be out of control. Now that we have dispelled these myths, you can take a more objective look at your child's behavior. Through the quiz, you have already identified some troublesome behavior patterns that could be linked to your child's diet. Now we're ready to explore more fully the symptoms of food-induced rudeness. By watching for and identifying these symptoms in your child if and when they turn up, you will be able to apply the advice in this book in an appropriate and timely manner.

What's more, following the dietary advice in this book will provide your child with an additional benefit besides stopping rude behavior: A more healthful diet can also strengthen the immune system and increase your child's resistance to germs and disease.

A happier kid. A healthier kid. A safer kid. And it all starts with the food that YOU provide!

identifying the symptoms of food-related rudeness

There are medical tests that can determine if a child's behavior is being influenced by the food he eats. We'll discuss them in detail in chapter 4. For the time being, however, we'll ask you to use that usually infallible diagnostic tool, a parent's power of observation. Take some time to carefully observe your child's eating habits and the kinds of behavior he shows after consuming certain foods.

Warning: Be objective! Don't let love cloud your vision. Too many parents and (especially) grandparents are so thrilled at the sight of a beloved child happily eating that they deny the possibility the food might have an adverse effect on the child later on.

Here's the basic approach you should take to determine the cause and cure for your child's bad attitude and rudeness.

1. Look for the symptoms described below.
2. Determine if there's a physiological condition that's causing the behavior problem (chapter 4).

3. Check to make sure your child's diet is meeting his basic nutritional needs (chapter 5).

4. Experiment with changes to your child's diet, starting by eliminating the worst foods and increasing the best foods (chapters 6 and 8).

5. Look beyond your child's nutrition into the behavioral conditions that may be causing his bad attitude and rudeness. Employ the proven three-step method to address different kinds of rudeness when you observe them (chapter 7).

6. Integrate these dietary and behavioral changes into your household with tactics that have worked for other parents and an approach that shows respect for your child and is designed on the findings of more than 2,000 studies of happy families (chapters 10 and 11).

Let's get started in this process by seeing if your child displays any of the following telltale signs of food-related rudeness.

Symptoms of Food-Related Rudeness

The following symptoms could signal real trouble now and may also be a sign of greater trouble in the years ahead.

Backtalk. While eating, or after eating, your child whines and disagrees rudely with everything you say. "No, I'm not taking the trash out right now. No, I am not going outside to get some fresh air. I don't have to do my homework now. No, I'm not turning off the TV," he says defiantly. He might also add that good old classic: "You can't make me do anything—you're not the boss of me!"

Fixation with snack food. Your child is too transfixed on food most of the time to care what you tell him. "Yeah?" he says with a shrug when you tell him about the traffic you encountered coming home from work. "So? Who cares?" He then dips into the bag of crunchy, cheesy snacks and brings up another large handful. "We're almost out of these things. We better not run out," he announces between chomps. "Except next time get me caramel corn, too, okay? And more chips, too."

Rudeness when eating. It is as though when this child is engaged in eating, all caring human characteristics have been put on hold. Gary, age 10, and his friend Roy were eating sandwich cookies, potato chips, and chocolate-flavored milk one afternoon when the phone call came telling Gary's dad that his mother (Gary's grandmother) had died. "Pish-em-wah!" Gary said to Roy on hearing this news from his father. Both boys started giggling then, took more bites of chips, and said "Pish-em-wah" over and over while Gary's father sobbed. Gary's mom came in just then, thankfully, and told the boys to stop acting in such an uncaring way. Gary's mom told me that normally, he is a very sensitive boy. "The only time he acts like he couldn't care less about anyone or anything is when he's stuffing himself with food!" she said.

Split personalities. Eighteen-year-old Lola was a normal eater who occasionally went out with friends for ice cream sundaes or banana splits. A lovely, helpful daughter to her mom and grandmother, who lived with the family and had helped raise her, Lola became a shrew after eating the ice cream treats. "You're fat!" she would yell at her plump grandmother out of the blue—in a voice dripping with hate. "You make me so ashamed. You never do your hair. Look, there's a spot on your dress. A food spot! I never want my friends to meet you—what will they think?" Later, after calming down, Lola would deny she had ever been so mean. "You're overreacting, Grandma," she'd say gently. "What you say I said just doesn't sound like me at all. Even if I did act like that, I didn't mean it. I just must have been in a really bad mood." Lola has since lost a few roommates in college from what she now suspects are food-caused attacks of verbal abuse.

Aggressiveness. I was part of a University of Arizona research project that studied recent intellectual, physical, emotional, and academic changes in today's children, as observed by teachers of students from kindergarten through high school. Many of the teachers that my colleagues and I interviewed reported that students' behavior is much more affected by eating habits than ever before. For instance, they said that students—especially those in the elementary grades—are far more likely to act out violently after eating lunch or certain snacks.

Parents have observed this phenomenon as well. Edna, mother of two children, a 6-year-old boy and a 10-year-old girl, saw it vividly in her family. After meals, Edna's daughter would pick fights with her brother that involved kicking, hitting, and slapping. "It's odd because she's really the gentler of the two of them," Edna said. "Usually, he's the one who's in trouble. But she can be really dangerous at certain times."

Sullenness. "Sullen" is a good description for a child who displays a kind of passive but persistent whininess that is never pleasant and often downright unappealing (to say the least). "No, I don't want to," is the sullen child's most common response. "How come I have to be the one you pick on?" and "I'm too tired" are also the kinds of things children say when they're being sullen. If food is causing a child to be sullen, it is causing him to feel exactly the way he acts: tired, put-upon, and very unhappy for reasons he cannot understand.

Paranoia. You don't have to be a psychologist to know that your child's angry cry of "You hate me! What are you looking at? You always make me feel like s—!" is a sign that she feels others are

?? ASK DR. CABIN ???????????

Q. *If I brought my daughter to you, how would you determine if she has a food-related behavior problem?*

A. Initially, I would take a history and perform a physical examination. The history would include a careful dietary history. I'd pay particular attention to your daughter's intake of sugar, artificial colors and flavors, preservatives, and chemicals. I would try to determine whether or not this is an allergic child, a sickly child, a malnourished child, an emotionally traumatized child, or a child with a compromised immune system. I would find out: Does she have mood swings, and are they associated with eating? Would she strangle for sugar or kill for caffeine?

On conducting a physical exam, I would determine if your daughter has signs of allergy, thrush, pallor, or a bloated abdomen. Does she relate to her parents? Does she suffer from an inability to concentrate, hyperactivity, tremor, subtle nystagmus (eye movement disturbance), or skin rashes?

Laboratory testing would include tests for thyroid disease, anemia, and deficiencies of vitamin B_{12}, folic acid, total protein, and albumin. If warranted, I might also test for food allergies, candida, hypoglycemia, or adrenal deficiencies.

Finally, if warranted, even more sophisticated homeopathic testing can be done as well as therapeutic trials of dietary changes and nutritional supplements.

against her. Yet some of the time, she can get along just fine with other people, displaying the ability to give and take that most kids use in socializing.

Sleepy rudeness. Your child gets really sleepy after eating certain foods—and is extremely rude upon first waking up. Michaela said that after dinner, her son Chad, 15, often falls fast asleep on the couch while doing his homework and "sleeps like the dead" for about an hour. "When he wakes up, he is so mean he is unbearable. He'll say, 'Mom! Why'd you let me sleep like that? You jerk! I told you I had all this homework to do!' And then he stays mean like that till he has a cup of coffee with lots of sugar and milk. I hate to let him have coffee at night, but it's the only way to stop that meanness!" The worst part—and what Michaela came to realize— is that Chad feels as awful as he is behaving. That sleepy rudeness, as I've come to call it, is one of the most unbearable kinds of rudeness a child can experience. There are few things worse than waking up hating the people around you.

Pessimism. Your child may be very pessimistic about life, people, school, and everything else. "You can't do that," he might say every time you suggest doing or trying something. Or he may feel he can't succeed at anything or that anything he wants to try will automatically fail. This negativity produces rudeness that is particularly debilitating because it attempts to undermine self-confidence in everyone subjected to it. "You can't lose that weight," Gary recently told his mother. "You know you can't. You tried before and look at you."

Belligerent cravings. Your child could suddenly behave like a drug addict. This behavior includes demanding certain foods immediately and driving everyone crazy until she gets them. She may appear to be happy while eating the demanded food, then act "high"—confused, sleepy, and insolent—afterward and become mean again until the next fix. Eating the food she craves just perpetuates this cycle until the child goes to sleep.

Hyper/sluggishness. Your child could behave like a speed freak. Parents who remember the behavior of diet-pill users in the 1960s and 1970s may be appalled to find their kids acting the same way. Eating seems to make the child happy and full of energy—for a while. When that phase ends, he becomes lazy, with an inability to do anything but complain about everything.

Understanding the Symptoms

The symptoms of food-related rudeness can vary greatly from child to child, depending on the child's metabolic rate, neurological makeup, and other physical characteristics. Some children may experience a variety of symptoms at different times; others may experience just one symptom. Further, the symptoms can range in degree from barely noticeable (you might think, "Hmm, that remark didn't sound like Billy!") to blatant, and from infrequent to very frequent in occurrence. In advanced cases of food-related rudeness, your child may become so overwhelmed by the foods' effects that he never really feels well or contented and is miserable (and making others miserable) all of the time.

Come on, you may be thinking skeptically, these behaviors are caused by kids who just want to give their parents a hard time. They are deliberately acting in these ways because they feel like it, and they can stop anytime they have a mind to.

I'm afraid that this is true in some cases. But I'm even more upset about the many cases where it's not true—where an otherwise good-natured kid is struggling, confused, or depressed by his own inexplicable mood swings and erratic behavior.

In the next chapter, you'll see how the body's reactions to certain foods can cause these awful behaviors. And you'll come to understand one of the primary messages of this book: Too many rude kids feel as terrible as they are behaving and are in need of nutritional help from their parents—and fast!

3

the unmistakable biological link between nutrition and behavior

Picturing how a car works can be a starting point to understanding how your child's body operates. In a car, the transmission,
cooling, and electrical systems all work together to support one another and keep the vehicle moving along smoothly. In a similar
way, according to Dr. Cabin, the circulatory, immune, nervous, respiratory, and other systems of your child's body work together to
keep him happy and healthy. While gas is the fuel for the car's engine, the food your child eats serves as the fuel for his body. Finally,
just as bad gasoline can "gum up" the car's engine, a poor diet can
cause your child's bodily systems to get out of balance.

Out of the 11 major systems in the body, 4 are directly influenced by a poor diet: the digestive, endocrine, nervous, and respiratory systems. When these systems malfunction as a result of
poor nutrition, they send your child's brain a biological "distress

signal" that something's wrong. The brain takes over, and the result is anger, mood swings, depression, abnormal fatigue (fatigue not resulting from normal physical and mental effort), apathy, and hostile behavior that may be uncontrollable, says Dr. Cabin. You see, the brain is capable of operating the body virtually on its own, according to an autonomous will, and of generating emotions that can be painful or pleasurable. Dr. Cabin explains that when your child's bodily systems aren't maintained properly, his brain's perceptions of everything, including persons, places, and things, change. The brain begins to interpret the child's world as dark, negative, threatening, dangerous, or just uninteresting and not worth the effort of respect or attention. In short, your child develops a "bad attitude" that results in rude behavior.

Because bad attitude and rude behaviors can also be caused by poor discipline, abuse, and other psychological conditions, food is seldom recognized by physicians as a contributing factor. Dr. Cabin has observed these destructive behaviors over the course of 20 years of medical practice, however, and he attributes them directly to poor nutrition and a breakdown in the ability of the body's systems to operate properly. Now, with the aid of this book, you will also come to understand how these attitudes and behaviors *can* be caused by diet—and, therefore, can be reversed by simple changes in what your child eats and drinks.

Children Are More Vulnerable

Children under the age of 12 can be especially vulnerable to diet-induced bad attitudes and rude behavior, says Dr. Cabin. That's because their bodies are still developing and growing, which makes getting the right varieties and quantities of nutrients even more essential than it is for adults. Yet many children tend to have poor diet and exercise habits (we'll address these issues in greater detail later on).

In addition, Dr. Cabin says that most children have what's known as a paradoxical response system, which means they can react differently to food and chemicals than adults. For example, consider the effect of caffeine or stimulant drugs on children. Instead of being made hyper by these substances, as adults would be, many children become more calm. Similarly, when kids are tired, they don't become sleepy and quiet, as adults would. Instead, they often become cranky and vociferous.

Finally, your child's genetic makeup and ethnic predisposition can increase his vulnerability to certain kinds of food even further.

Food: The Fuel for Good Behavior

The digestive, endocrine, nervous, and respiratory systems are designed to work together to keep your child on an even keel. With proper nutrition, they function correctly, releasing optimum amounts of nutrients, hormones, and oxygen to power your child's body and brain, which keeps him in control of his emotions and behavior. Not too hyper. Not too lethargic. Not too aggressive. Not too cynical.

The quality of your child's diet affects every one of these systems, though, and in turn, it alters the measure of control that these systems have over your child's brain activity and state of mind.

If his digestion is sluggish, his digestive system sends out a signal to his brain that something is wrong. If his metabolism is overrun by sugar surges or caffeine rushes, other distress signals are activated, as neurotransmitters (substances such as dopamine and serotonin that regulate mood) and hormones kick in frantically and ineffectively to try to bring stability back to his brain.

Even your child's ability to properly take in oxygen is affected by food, since his breathing relies on a vigorous, nutrition-powered immune system to defend his body against airborne toxins, says Dr. Cabin. On an even more fundamental level, a healthy diet is necessary for the efficient use and exchange of oxygen by the cells. This is a complex metabolic process known as cellular respiration, or cellular "breathing." A good diet causes healthy cells, and healthy cells are far more capable of maintaining and easily carrying out this process than unhealthy cells.

Only when they're working together, and properly fueled by healthy eating, can your child's bodily systems give him the proper brain balance to retain his composure, accept direction and discipline from you, and keep a cheerful outlook on life.

Now let's take a closer look at how diet affects each of your child's key systems.

How Your Child Digests Food

As your child eats, digestive enzymes break down the food and allow the nutrients in the food to be absorbed by your child's body. Indigestible fiber and the remaining food residue is passed from her body as waste. Problems develop, however, when her diet consists of highly processed, low-fiber foods that slow digestion and cause buildups of waste in her body.

According to Dr. Cabin, this buildup leads to constipation and can trigger anxiety and despair. What's more, foods containing antibiotics, such as nonorganic dairy products and meats, can kill off the good intestinal flora that helps the body assimilate nutrients during digestion. This imbalance creates the perfect environment for yeast infections, which are often associated with a chronic sense of apathy, depression, lethargy, malaise, and ennui.

Reverse Rudeness with Better Digestion

Best foods to improve digestion: Herbs, such as licorice, anise, fennel, turmeric, garlic, ginger, and aloe. Give these to your child in teas, or put ground herbs in shakers and allow your child to sprinkle them on her food (store the shakers in the refrigerator). These herbs have been used by many cultures for thousands of years. Curry, for instance, contains turmeric, garlic, and ginger.

Foods to avoid: Greasy or fatty foods, overprocessed foods (those listing mostly chemicals and trans fatty acids on the labels), white flour, white sugar, high-fat cheeses, coffee, and red meat.

How Your Child Metabolizes Food

The endocrine system is a series of glands and organs that secrete small amounts of potent hormones that regulate much of the body's processes, including metabolism, or the use of food for fuel. This system consists of glands—the thyroid, hypothalamus, parathyroid, pituitary, and adrenal glands—as well as several organs with endocrine tissue, such as the pancreas. The adrenal glands, for example, secrete hormones that help to regulate your reaction to stress, while the pancreas has endocrine tissue that helps to regulate blood sugar.

The endocrine system needs essential fatty acids, proteins, and vitamins and minerals such as vitamin C, selenium, zinc, magnesium, manganese, molybdenum, and copper. Fish and flaxseed are good sources of essential fatty acids, while beans, nuts, and seeds are healthful sources of protein. Sea salt is a good source of iodine and other trace minerals. Vegetables such as broccoli and sweet potatoes are high in vitamin C.

Low Blood Sugar

Does this pattern of behavior sound familiar? Your child eats food that is very high in sugar, like pudding with whipped cream. After the initial euphoria, she becomes grumpy and lethargic and craves more sugary snacks, but eating them just triggers a repeat of this behavior. This cycle is interrupted only by drowsiness and heavy sleep. Yet when she wakes up, she feels worse, is even more rude and difficult to be with, and craves a sugar "fix" all over again.

If this sounds like your child, she is showing the typical signs of reactive hypoglycemia, or low blood sugar, a condition that occurs when the pancreas is overloaded with sugar. The pancreas is enormously influential on mood because it regulates levels of the hormone insulin. Insulin stimulates the uptake of sugar from the bloodstream into the cells to be used as fuel for energy. A diet high in sugar and refined foods, such as that eaten by many American children, eventually exhausts the ability of the pancreas to regulate insulin supply, thereby causing lack of blood sugar in the cells. The

Reverse Rudeness by Regulating Blood Sugar

Best foods and practices to balance insulin: Frequent consumption of small meals containing protein and complex carbohydrates such as whole grains, legumes, fruits, and vegetables. This food regimen keeps the pancreas working smoothly to produce insulin in normal amounts.

Foods to avoid: Refined carbohydrates, such as syrups, white sugar, and flour, which are stripped of the "packaging" nature intended.

effect on the brain and behavior is dramatic and instant: anxiety, panic, suspicion of others' intentions, despair, hostility, and pessimism.

You may also notice your child suffering from "sick" fatigue—the kind that, as someone I know who has low blood sugar puts it, renders one too tired to even try to be cooperative. No matter how much you demand your child's help in picking up her toys or doing her chores, she seems incapacitated. This can cause her to feel guilty and shameful. "People would think I was defective in character—just too lazy to be believed, when that laziness came over me," a sufferer explained. "They didn't understand it was physical, caused by what I ate. But thanks to changes in what I eat and when, I almost never suffer from this laziness anymore."

Other symptoms produced by blood sugar imbalance include poor memory, confusion, and an inability to learn new material—or process material already known. It's as though your child's IQ has been suddenly lowered, and in a way, it actually has been because her brain is disoriented by the insulin imbalance.

Stress

The adrenal gland affects moods because it produces hormones, such as cortisol, that are designed to help your child handle stress. These hormones enable her to deal with crises, such as deadline pressures, sports competitions, and relationship dramas. After an initial rush of these hormones, your child should be able to regain control of her personality and be able to think and act clearly.

Problems can occur when her system is repeatedly "tricked" into overreacting by foods that trigger adrenaline, particularly caffeine and sugar. After this temporary "high," your child may experience jittery nerves and a lack of concentration.

How Your Child's Brain Works

Your child's nervous system consists of the brain and the nerves leading from the brain to the spinal cord and all parts of the body. Her brain operates by the use of neurotransmitters—such as serotonin and dopamine—that transmit electrical impulses. Your child's diet can either enhance these connections and improve her performance and sense of well-being, or it can reduce the clarity of these connections and lead to poor attention and concentration.

An important connection between a child's diet and how well his brain functions was made in the 1970s. That's when Benjamin Feingold, M.D., chief of pediatrics at Cedars of Lebanon Hospital in Los Angeles until he retired at age 81 as chief emeritus of the department of allergy at Kaiser Permanente Medical Center in San Francisco, and such colleagues as Dr. Stephen D. Locky Sr., of the Mayo Clinic, developed an elimination diet as a treatment for asthma, learning difficulties, behavioral problems, and bed-wetting, among other conditions in children. They discovered that some naturally occurring chemicals, such as salicylate (the ingredient in aspirin that is also found in apples and other foods), affected the aforementioned symptoms in kids, and that artificially added ingredients, such as food dyes and preservatives, also contributed to a reduced ability to learn, concentrate, sleep well, sit still, and perform other functions. In fact, Dr. Feingold reported more than 300 symptoms of behavioral and learning problems that may be linked to synthetic additives and salicylates.

Children given diets eliminating the offending substances were said to be on the "Feingold diet," and soon the Feingold diet and Dr. Feingold's ideas became well-known. Even though many other medical experts have since come to agree and practice the Feingold dietary principles, they allow the Feingold name to stand for those beliefs and practices. While early studies did not find a conclusive link between diet and behavior, the newer ones are far more supportive. Enough parents and medical authorities have been impressed by the diet's effectiveness to form the Feingold Association, a nonprofit international organization that now provides a Web site (www.feingold.org), conferences, newsletters, and other services.

While Dr. Feingold's behavioral interest was mainly in the area

Reverse Rudeness by Boosting Brainpower

Best foods for improving brain function: Foods high in amino acids, such as fish, lean meat and poultry, beans, and soy, can improve neurotransmitter operation and produce feelings of well-being. (Turkey, which is high in the "feel good" amino acid tryptophan, is an especially good choice.) Essential fatty acids, found in fish, leafy green vegetables, and canola and sunflower oil, are critical to the nervous system, which relies on them for cell membrane and brain development.

Foods to avoid: Sugar, processed carbohydrates, artificial flavors, chemical flavor enhancers, colors, sweeteners, protein isolates, and monosodium glutamate (MSG).

of learning disorders, such as what is now known as Attention Deficit Disorder and Attention Deficit Hyperactivity Disorder, his work can certainly be connected to rude behavior in kids. Children who cannot settle down enough to learn are often thought of as rude and difficult. A recent study published in *The Journal of Pediatrics* reported that irritable behavior in 150 of 200 children improved on a diet free of synthetic food coloring. Surely, "irritable" behavior is synonymous with rude behavior in many children! Many other studies on the effects of diet on learning and attention in children are discussed on the Feingold Association Web site.

How Your Child Breathes

Your child's respiratory system includes the nose, nasal passages, lungs, and bronchial tubes that branch off into about 300 million places in her body. This system takes the oxygen she breathes, puts it into the red blood cells, and takes away the carbon dioxide that she exhales.

Without proper nutrition, your child's immune system weakens. This will actually reduce her body's capacity to take in and process fresh oxygen. Poor oxygen intake has been shown to result in depression, low energy, and reduced enjoyment of life. Continued weakening of the immune system with nutrient-poor foods can contribute to respiratory ailments such as chronic bronchitis, which further limit your child's ability to enjoy an active, healthy lifestyle.

How Much Longer Can Your Family Wait for This Answer?

Despite all the scientific evidence (see "Ask Dr. Cabin" on page 42), many people are still under the false impression that food

Reverse Rudeness by Increasing Oxygen Intake

Best foods to boost respiratory function: The respiratory system needs the antioxidants—vitamins C, E, and beta-carotene as well as zinc and selenium. Excellent sources of these nutrients include whole grains, leafy green vegetables, carrots, squash, yams, nuts, and seeds, plus orange fruits, such as citrus and melon.

Foods to avoid: Sugar, artificial colors, sweeteners, preservatives, refined carbohydrates, tobacco, and drugs.

has little or nothing to do with a child's behavior. In fact, we probably all know some very successful, seemingly healthy people who grew up on fried mayonnaise sandwiches, sweet iced tea, pecan pie, hand-dipped ice cream, and flapjacks. There may be supreme court justices, CEOs, heroic firefighters, and beautiful actresses who have eaten whatever they wanted and, because of some lucky break of genetics, never known the debilitating effects of food-induced rudeness, depression, confusion, or aggression.

Sadly, though, there are also millions, make that tens of millions, of children today who are needlessly suffering with emotional flare-ups, poor self-esteem, feelings of inadequacy, depression, and anger simply because they've never been taught the right way to eat. Their behavior may even be exacerbated by a genetic condition that makes them particularly prone to the behavior-altering effects of food. The fact that you picked up this book shows that you think you may have one of these children in your home right now. Your child may be waiting for you to find

?? ASK DR. CABIN ?? ?? ?? ?? ?? ?

Q. *What scientific evidence most convinces you of the connection between diet and a child's attitude and behavior?*

A. The observation of the relationship between food and mood in children goes back to ancient times, when Greek physicians Hippocrates and Galen concluded that health was related to diet and other observable factors, rather than edicts of the gods.

The pioneering work of Theron Randolph, M.D., with whom I had the great privilege of working, opened my eyes to the effects of food allergies and yeast-related problems on children's behavior. His colleague, psychiatrist William Philpott, M.D., also influenced me by outlining changes in behavior related to food in his classic book, *Brain Allergies: The Psychonutrient Connection.* Dr. Randolph and his contemporaries, especially Sherry Rogers, M.D., and Doris Rapp, M.D., have published numerous studies that clearly show the relationships between diet and behaviors. Two pediatricians, William Crook, M.D., and Benjamin Feingold, M.D., have also published influential books on the relationships between food and mood.

Finally, my own personal experience with hundreds of patients, as well as family members and friends, has solidified this connection between diet and attitude and behavior beyond a shadow of a doubt in my mind.

the answer that can help her live the happy life she deserves.

The rest of this book will help you act in simple yet powerful ways to improve your child's outlook on life and bring your whole family the peace and happiness for which you've been waiting.

part 2

Solutions That Reverse Rudeness

4

food cures

When food is behind your child's bad attitude and rudeness, it's often because he suffers from a physiological condition that puts his body under abnormal stress. This chapter presents a list of the most common conditions that can trigger this reaction and explains how to tell whether your child might suffer from one or more of them. For each condition, you'll find practical strategies that you can use to help your child overcome the symptoms he's experiencing and ease their effect on his attitude and behavior.

Hypoglycemia

Also called low blood sugar, this condition is perhaps the most powerful cause of rudeness and bad attitude in kids—and adults, for that matter, according to Dr. Cabin. It's not a disease, but rather a response by the body to the consumption of certain foods. Symptoms of hypoglycemia can be temporary and occasional, resulting just after certain foods are eaten, or constant and chronic, forcing the person to avoid certain foods for life.

Hypoglycemia can be triggered in your child when he eats sugary foods or carbohydrates. Refined sugar (found in especially high amounts in soda, cake icings, cotton candy, and chocolate) and refined carbs (found in such foods as pastries, cookies, pasta, biscuits, and dumplings) are the usual culprits, but natural fruit sugars (found in all fruits but especially in ripe bananas, grapes, figs, watermelon, and other very sweet fruits) can also be potent triggers, as can all the different forms of honey.

Hypoglycemia's effect on behavior is most severe during the time when your child's body is in between "sugar highs." Overworked by a rush of sugar, his pancreas releases insulin that prevents too much sugar from circulating in the bloodstream, explains Dr. Cabin. This makes his body desperately crave more sweets and carbs to boost its blood sugar levels. The end result? Your child feels awful, hostile, and aggressive until he gets more.

The most alarming aspect of hypoglycemia, says Dr. Cabin, is its capacity for perpetuating itself. The craving for more sugar caused by the drop in blood sugar levels sets up an addiction cycle. Your child's body is immediately gratified when he eats a cookie or drinks some soda. All his bad feelings are instantly relieved. But relief is only temporary and powers the bad attitude cycle all over again. If denied the sugar fix, your child's body can go on craving it for as long as 5 days, according to Dr. Cabin. Even if you are able to break your child of this cycle, an innocent dessert from a favorite aunt or a birthday party at school can get it going again in full force.

The potential dangers of hypoglycemia have been understood for years, but they're often overlooked by today's pediatricians. This is especially unfortunate because the trend toward a diet rich in refined sugars and carbs makes hypoglycemia very common.

The main reason why many physicians fail to recognize hypoglycemia in their patients is that the condition is difficult to diagnose precisely. The medical test is time-consuming, often inconclusive, and always expensive to do. It involves fasting and in-office testing via intravenous tubes—not something you'd want to subject your child to unless it's absolutely necessary.

Even if you don't have your child tested for chronic hypoglycemia, though, it's easy to observe if his behavior is following the kind of pattern described above. If it is, you can modify his diet to lessen the condition's rudeness-causing effects.

Hypoglycemia can affect its victims for their lifetimes. But its miserable symptoms can be eased, or even eliminated, by changes in diet. Your child will need to learn to eat certain foods at certain times and avoid others completely. With the changes prescribed below (and additional changes that your nutritionist or pediatrician might add), you should notice an improvement in your child's mood and behavior within 5 days. If these changes do not help brighten your child's attitude by then, consider that he might be cheating on the diet when he's with friends or that he might be hitting the vending machines at school. (Strategies suggested in later chapters will help you deal with that problem.)

Feed him like a cow. "Eating small, frequent meals, often called grazing, is the best strategy," says Dr. Cabin. "Give your child some food every 3 to 4 hours with an emphasis on protein." Eating this way will keep blood sugar levels from dropping and will maintain a steady supply of fuel. It also boosts the metabolism, which helps control your child's weight.

Eat the whole thing. Vegetables, whole grains, fresh nuts and seeds, and small amounts of low-carb fruits are nutritious whole foods that will help regulate blood sugar, according to Dr. Cabin.

Meat me for protein. "It's especially important to eat protein-rich fish, such as salmon, trout, haddock, bass, and catfish—unfarmed, if possible. Avoid the fish most likely to contain mercury, such as tuna and swordfish. Herring are great, in the form of sardines (fresh, not smoked) and fish steaks," says Dr. Cabin. "Chicken and other lean meats are also good sources of protein, but look for meat that has been raised without antibiotics or hormones," he notes.

Protein eaten in small quantities every few hours keeps hypoglycemia at bay by keeping blood sugar levels even. Think of protein use this way: We humans are mammals, made of animal protein. Eating other animal proteins, such as meat and eggs, in small amounts on frequent and regular occasions will provide the amino acids we are made of and need in order to function at our best. We need amino acids, for instance, to make the neurotransmitters that are so essential for feelings of well-being and to allow our endocrine systems to regulate the insulin that is so important in keeping our blood sugar levels from getting out of control.

Go easy on the soy. "Soy products, such as meatless hamburger and soy milk, are good sources of protein," notes Dr. Cabin. "But serve them to your child in moderation, and look for organic products." No more than one meal a day should offer soy as the main protein source. The other meals should offer complete proteins from animal sources, such as lean beef, chicken, eggs, yogurt, or, for children who can tolerate it, low-fat or fat-free milk. (For more on soy, see chapter 6.)

Enjoy the good fats. "All fats are not bad. Certain fats are considered good and should be included in your child's diet," says Dr. Cabin. These good fats include monounsaturated fats (olive and

canola oils and macadamia nuts, peanuts, pecans
and polyunsaturated fats (corn oil, safflower oil, soybe
etable oils). Saturated fats (found in meat, dairy prodi
should be limited, and hydrogenated fats (margarine   vegetable
shortening) should be eliminated entirely. This is sound advice for
everyone, not just children.

Emphasize the essential fatty acids. A kind of polyunsaturated
fatty acid found in fish, walnuts, and flaxseed, omega-3 has been
shown to have a wide range of health benefits for the heart, skin,
joints, and respiratory system. Research also suggests that consuming omega-3s might influence the production of the brain's
feel-good neurotransmitter serotonin and may reduce depression
and aggressive behavior.

In addition, a study conducted in the department of foods and
nutrition at Purdue University found that 53 children diagnosed
with Attention Deficit Hyperactivity Disorder (ADHD) had significantly lower concentrations of key fatty acids in their bodies than
did 43 control-group children who did not have ADHD. The reason
why ADHD is often linked to a lack of essential fatty acids in the
body is still not well understood.

While the research on essential fatty acids is preliminary, it does
suggest that shifting your child's diet from saturated and hydrogenated fats to omega-3 fatty acids can help improve her mood.

If you buy fatty acids in capsule or oil form, make sure they are
cold or expeller pressed, not hydrogenated. If the oil smells rancid
when you open the bottle, return it to the store right away. Never
consume rancid oils, no matter how much you paid. Refrigerate
oils and capsules after opening the bottle to keep them from becoming rancid.

Avoid the poison. It's best to think of all foods with high amounts of refined carbohydrates as poison to your child. This includes all sugar, sweets, sodas, white flour products, and, sadly, an excess of fruits. These are the very foods that can be the instant triggers for your child's worst behaviors.

For more information on hypoglycemia, write to the Hypoglycemia Association, Box 165, Ashton, MD, 20861-0165. You can listen to a recorded message with information on the organization at (202) 544-4044.

Constipation

Constipation can make kids *feel* bad in ways that make them *act* bad—rude, sullen, irritable, and negative about everything. The most common causes of constipation are lack of natural fiber in the diet and dehydration, caused by drinking too little water. Other, less common causes include hypothyroidism, inactivity, genetic factors, a change in normal bacteria in the colon, and certain medications.

How do you know if your child is suffering from constipation? Just check the toilet. His bowel movement should be large, float, be well-formed, and shouldn't have a strong odor. Optimally, he could have up to three bowel movements a day, but no fewer than one a day.

To find out if constipation is adversely affecting your child's behavior, try some of the remedies below and see if he feels and acts better after a few days. Ask your child if going to the bathroom has become easier and more complete. If your child's constipation is not remedied by these dietary changes in about 3 days, a physical exam might be in order. You may want to have him tested for intestinal blockages and other conditions that can be more serious.

Go the whole way. The simplest and most fundamental way to ease constipation is to increase the amount of vegetables and whole grains like brown rice and barley in your child's diet. As he gets more and more of his calories from whole foods, and fewer from refined foods, his digestion will markedly improve.

Think long-term. Unless your doctor tells you otherwise, your child's constipation means that he is eating foods that have too few nutrients and too little fiber and not drinking enough water. So, for a long-term solution, you have to permanently change his diet. "Add more fiber from apples, figs, sunflower and pumpkin seeds, and raw vegetables such as carrots," suggests Dr. Cabin.

Add water. If your child doesn't take in enough water, his digestive system can become sluggish. "Your young school-age child should be drinking eight 8-ounce glasses of water per day, increasing to twelve glasses by the time he's a teenager," notes Dr. Cabin. "And if he's playing sports that cause him to perspire heavily, his intake should be increased to at least 4 ounces every 20 minutes, with 10 to 12 ounces consumed a half-hour before the athletic activity begins."

Avoid store-bought laxatives. "Commercial laxatives are too harsh on your child's intestinal system," warns Dr. Cabin. "Plus, you don't want to think of this as a short-term problem that can be fixed overnight."

Sample some psyllium. "You can try psyllium husk or powder added to food twice a day accompanied always by a glass of water. Psyllium is a powerful bowel regulator, but it can ball up and cause constipation if it's not taken with a large amount of water," notes Dr. Cabin.

He advises against buying commercial products with psyllium in them since they are often loaded with sugar and other additives your child doesn't need.

Prune away the problem. "Your child can naturally relieve his symptoms of constipation by drinking a small glass of prune juice at night or eating two or three prunes or figs, taken with at least 16 ounces of water," says Dr. Cabin.

Decaffeinate your child. "Cut back on beverages that contain caffeine, such as soda and coffee," recommends Dr. Cabin. Caffeine dehydrates all parts of the body, including the walls of the intestinal tract through which nutrient molecules are supposed to pass. This causes a pileup in your child's colon, causing discomfort of the kind that can make him feel and act mean and depressed.

Candidiasis

Though "candidiasis" sounds scary, it's actually a type of yeast infection. It's caused by the fungus *Candida albicans*, a yeast that naturally occurs in the human body. If this fungus grows beyond normal levels, it can create misery by releasing its waste products in the bowel, say some physicians, including Dr. Cabin. According to these doctors, these waste products then get absorbed into the child's bloodstream and travel throughout the body, making her feel—and act—depressed. Symptoms can become so severe that the child has a bad attitude most of her waking hours.

How can a child get this condition? Usually, by taking antibiotics or steroids. Antibiotics kill off not only the disease-causing germs but also the good bacteria in the digestive tract that keep the *Candida* fungus at bay. Without these good bacteria, the yeast can take over. It feeds on sugar, so your child can also get candidiasis by eating too much sugar (particularly if she has undiagnosed diabetes).

Besides rude behavior and a bad attitude, your child will probably show some physical signs of the condition. According to Drs. Mark and Angela Stengler, authors of the book *Your Vital Child*, symptoms cover five major areas of the body and include the skin (excessive sweating, acne, psoriasis, eczema, and hives), the nervous system (hyperactivity, anxiety, moodiness, extreme fatigue, forgetfulness, sleeplessness, and, in extreme cases, hallucinations and violent behavior), the digestive system (bloating, cramps, food allergies, gas, and swings between bouts of diarrhea and constipation), the endocrine system (hypothyroidism and hyperthyroidism), and the genitourinary tract (for boys, anal or rectal itching, genital rashes, and jock itch; for girls, bloating, cramps, bladder or vaginal infections, and mood swings, particularly in those who have reached puberty).

Treatments include the following.

Ointment on the outside. Schedule an appointment with your child's pediatrician. Treatment will probably include antifungal creams and medication, according to Dr. Cabin.

Yogurt on the inside. Dr. Cabin believes that candidiasis should also be treated with plain yogurt, which contains good bacteria, called acidophilus, that will fight and kill off the bad fungi. If your child won't eat yogurt, you can buy acidophilus in liquid or capsule form at health food stores. The liquid probably works the fastest and best, Dr. Cabin adds. There are several brands available, and all should be kept refrigerated in the store and at home. Good, additive-free yogurt can be purchased at any supermarket. Organic brands such as Stonyfield Farm are widely available.

Cut off the supply. Don't give your child sugar in any form, warns Dr. Cabin. Also avoid moldy foods (such as cheese), peanuts, pistachios, vinegar, pickled foods, fruit juices, white commercial mushrooms, malt, commercial lunchmeats, smoked foods, and

(continued on page 56)

DR. CABIN'S
Nutritional Breakthroughs

Low-Carb, No-Sugar Diet Brings Blessed Relief to Twins and Mom:

Regina, Nora, and Nicky's Story

Regina was a young mother when she first consulted Dr. Cabin. She had been plagued with infections her entire life, mainly recurrent strep tonsillitis requiring lots of doses of antibiotics. Now, at the age of 26, Regina was the mother of 5-week-old twins, Nora and Nicky. Ecstatic about this new turn of events in her life, she was thrilled that God had blessed her with not just one but two darling babies.

Now, Regina was not so much worried about her own health, which was hardly robust, but that of her twins. Nora and Nicky had both suffered from painful thrush (an oral yeast rash) around and in their little mouths, as well as difficult dispositions—constant crying and fretting and other signs of unhappiness—since birth. Plus, they were not gaining anywhere near enough weight even though Regina was breast-feeding.

Dr. Cabin's tests of Regina revealed that she had high levels of antibodies to the fungus *Candida albicans*, and he diagnosed her with systemic candidiasis. This condition was almost certainly caused by all the antibiotics Regina had taken over the years. While they had killed the disease-causing bacteria, they had also destroyed the "good" bacteria that would normally have kept the *Candida* fungus in check. Dr. Cabin explained that the candidiasis had been passed on to the children through her breast milk. That was why they, too, showed the malaise and thrush symptoms at such young ages. Poor little things!

Regina was willing to do anything that would allow her to go on breastfeeding and readily agreed to Dr. Cabin's dietary rules: a low-carbohydrate, no-sugar, no-yeast diet and an oral antifungal medication. After 4 weeks, the twins' moods improved markedly, as did their weight and appetites. Further, their thrush rashes disappeared for good!

Here's one final—and amazing—note to this case history: After following Dr. Cabin's dietary recommendations, Regina stopped getting strep infections and so went months without having to take antibiotics. Only when she relapsed and went back to eating sugar and carbs did she contract a strep infection again. She has since learned her lesson—that her old diet weakens her already challenged immune system—and has vowed not to relapse again.

large amounts of fruit (more than two pieces a day). Adults with candidiasis should also avoid alcohol.

Food Dye Sensitivities

The effect of food dyes and additives remains a controversial subject among pediatricians. Dr. Cabin, for one, is a firm believer that they can make children uncontrollably rude, even hyper.

Joe Ahuero of Tucson, the father of a 3-year-old boy, has seen it with his own eyes. "Whenever my boy eats anything red or even pink, like candy or a drink or a piece of cake, he's bouncing off the walls for a couple of hours," notes Joe. According to Dr. Cabin, food dyes can inflame the nervous systems of some children. The inflamed nerves can in turn make the children feel and act hyper.

Some of the most famous work on the effect of food dyes on children was done by Benjamin Feingold, M.D., a professor of pediatrics at Northwestern University Medical School in Chicago who later became chief of pediatrics at Cedars of Lebanon Hospital in Los Angeles. In the 1970s, Dr. Feingold found that symptoms of learning disabilities and a lack of emotional control associated with what's now known as Attention Deficit Disorder (ADD) were seen in children who ate foods containing sugar, artificial colors and flavors, and salicylates (naturally occurring aspirin-like substances). When he removed these foods from the children's diets, he found that their symptoms improved. Many researchers have since maintained that Dr. Feingold's work is invalid and that Ritalin and similar drugs are the only effective remedies for ADD symptoms. Dr. Cabin disagrees and maintains that Dr. Feingold's work was an important step forward in understanding children's behavior.

The Yale Guide to Children's Nutrition lists yellow dye #5 (tartrazine) as a possible cause of behavior problems in kids, including irritability, restlessness, and sleep disturbances. But the book adds that studies researching its effects have been criticized for "methodological flaws." Dr. Cabin asserts that other food dyes, such as red dye #3 (erythrosine), citrus red #2, yellow dye #6, green dye #3, blue dye #1 and #2, and red dye #40 can produce the same behavior changes as those attributed to tartrazine.

In her practice, Doris Rapp, M.D., a pediatric allergist, has associated food dyes not just with behavior problems, but also with confused thinking in kids. She discusses her findings at length in her book *Is This Your Child?*

Become a detective. How do you know if your child's behavior is being influenced by food dyes? Observation is the key, according to both Dr. Cabin and Dr. Rapp. When your child's rudeness seems to include hyperactive behavior, find out if he has had any foods recently that contained dyes, say, in breakfast cereals or goodies at a school party. Be rigorous in your investigation. Since the smallest amounts of dyes are often enough to trigger some kids' rudeness and bad attitude, it can be difficult to pinpoint which food was responsible, or if there were several. If you suspect this is a problem for your child, you might want to contact the Feingold Association (www.feingold.org) for a list of foods that are free of dyes.

Look over the label. If you suspect that your child has a problem with food dye sensitivity, be vigilant about checking food labels and avoid giving him food that contains artificial colors and flavors, recommends Dr. Cabin. Natural colorings, such as those from beets, strawberries, and carrots, can be blended into icings and cookies to add not just color but more nourishment as well.

Vitamin and Mineral Deficiencies

Certain vitamins and minerals play a role in keeping your child's mood stable. The B vitamins are particularly known for their positive effects on mood, while the major "feel good" minerals are calcium, magnesium, and iron. Children deficient in these nutrients are likely to be grumpy and rude most of the time and unable to control their behavior.

The list of benefits of the B vitamins is long and varied. Vitamin B_6 is the precursor of the amino acid tryptophan, that much-touted natural tranquilizer that provides your child with a sense of calm; vitamin B_{12} promotes a sense of being energized integrated with a feeling of well-being; folic acid and niacin have been associated with learning abilities and intelligence in kids.

Other research suggests that low levels of certain vitamins (B_1, B_2, niacin, folic acid, B_{12}, and vitamins C and D) and minerals (calcium, iron, magnesium, selenium, and zinc) can cause depression, irritability, or mood swings.

It's reasonable to suspect vitamin deficiencies in your child if she has a poor appetite, shows apathetic and whiny rudeness most of the time, has more of a sad than bad attitude, and shows a general unhealthy, pale color in her face. A good doctor is the best person to test for vitamin deficiencies.

Think food first. The best way to make sure your child gets all of the vitamins and minerals she needs is to provide her with a healthful diet of fresh, whole foods. For B vitamins, serve green, leafy vegetables and whole grains. Excellent sources of calcium include dairy foods, raw endive, watercress, kale, navy beans, almonds, sunflower seeds, and walnuts. For magnesium, serve your child apples, soybeans, figs, lemons, almonds, sunflower and sesame seeds, brown rice, and green, leafy vegetables such as kale, endive, chard, celery, and beet tops. To ensure adequate iron intake, give your child raisins, dark green vegetables, and an occasional tablespoonful of blackstrap molasses. (Just be sure to have your child brush her teeth after eating this molasses. While it

packs a powerful nutritional wallop, it can decay her
if not brushed off immediately.)

Then, a multi. If you believe your child's diet isn't gi
full lineup of the vitamins and minerals she needs, you can make
sure she gets them with a multivitamin. (*Note:* If you suspect that
your child might have an iron deficiency, consult your pediatrician,
who can then prescribe an iron supplement at the best dosage. Be
particularly careful about adhering to the dosage, since excessive
iron intake can be deadly in children.)

Nature creates nutrients in balanced complexes (which is why
food sources are best), and Dr. Cabin recommends only those vitamin and mineral products that have been balanced as carefully as
possible. He has formulated several vitamin products that can be
ordered by mail (see page 204 for details). Otherwise, look for multivitamins that are free of additives, dyes, and preservatives. They
should contain vitamins A, C, E, K, and the Bs—1, 2, 3, 6, 12, d-3,
folate, and biotin—as well as magnesium, calcium, potassium,
zinc, manganese, copper, chromium, molybdenum, and selenium.
Make sure the brand you buy is labeled for children; you can find
acceptable brands in reputable health food stores and some supermarkets.

Caffeine Sensitivity

In amounts exceeding 60 milligrams, caffeine can make children
feel out of control, hostile, and suspicious, says Dr. Cabin. They
then act out these feelings by misbehaving. Unfortunately, it
doesn't take much to consume this amount of caffeine: A 12-ounce
can of Mountain Dew contains 55 milligrams of caffeine; a can of
Coca Cola contains 47 milligrams, and a can of Pepsi contains 39.
Further, children who are especially sensitive to caffeine will start

behaving badly after consuming just a tiny amount, such as that smidgen found in decaffeinated tea or coffee, or in chocolate bars.

Children get literally addicted to caffeine by taking in more caffeine to ease the symptoms they begin to suffer when the last jolt of caffeine begins to wear off. When, for instance, the effect of one caffeinated soda begins wearing off, the child wants another to forestall the drop in spirits he feels. The parent, not knowing what is going on, usually gives him this new soda without thinking.

Here's how to pull the plug on caffeine.

Go cold turkey. Testing for caffeine sensitivity is simple. Just remove all sources of caffeine (which means reading food labels for listings) and observe your child's behavior for about 4 days.

Be aware that your child's behavior might not change immediately. His body may need 24 to 72 hours to be detoxified of all caffeine. During this "detox" period, he could endure actual withdrawal symptoms, so be prepared to comfort him and to assure him that he'll feel better in just another few days. Soothe his erratic thoughts and impulses, and if he feels unable to concentrate, assure him that this feeling will pass as well. When the detoxing is done, your child should have a whole new positive attitude and be able to sleep well at night.

Practice zero tolerance. Dr. Cabin stresses that kids should avoid caffeinated sodas at all costs. Unless your doctor or pharmacist insists, your child should also avoid over-the-counter medicines that contain caffeine.

Substitute. Provide caffeine-free foods as substitutes for caffeine-laden foods. That means Postum or other cereal-like beverages instead of coffee, herb tea instead of regular or decaffeinated tea, and fruit drinks and juices instead of caffeinated sodas.

Chuck the chocolate. Remove all chocolate from your child's diet, as well as coffee-flavored foods, which may contain traces of caffeine.

Take precautions outside your home. Warn hosts of birthday parties, sleepovers, and other events that your child should not be given anything with caffeine. In addition, train your child to search food labels for that ingredient as soon as he's old enough to recognize the word.

Eating Disorders

The pressure to be thin and beautiful is everywhere—even for children. Kids feel they have to watch their weight to make the team, fit in with their friends, or wear the latest hip-hugging fashions. As a result, eating disorders such as anorexia, bulimia, and binge eating seem to be affecting children at increasingly young ages. These are serious conditions that require treatment by experienced medical professionals. One sign that your child might have an eating disorder is a change in behavior. Your once pleasant daughter or son may suddenly become rude, sullen, and secretive. These behavioral changes are a result not only of basic hunger but also of vitamin, mineral, and protein deficiencies.

A mom I'll call Becky, the parent of a 6-year-old girl in Southern California, said she was so appalled at the thin-as-a-rail body standards for the other little girls in her daughter's dance class that she withdrew her daughter from the class. "My little girl is on the chunky side, but she's very healthy and happy," this mom said. "But after a few sessions of this ballet class, she began to feel really bad about the way she looked and to talk about having to lose a lot of weight. No way would I even let her diet at her age!"

In addition to self-esteem issues such as those Becky witnessed, studies on children who failed to get proper nutrition suggest that behavior impairments associated with early malnutrition can have long-term effects. These impairments can include learning difficulties, an unwillingness to deal with authority, a poor social life, an inability to concentrate, and in general, the inability to function in school, at home, and later, as a successful employee, spouse, and parent. Children with eating disorders can certainly suffer from a lack of nutrition for as long as their disorders are allowed to continue.

To help prevent eating disorders in your family, follow the strategies below.

Talk. The most important thing a parent can do to prevent eating disorders, says Dr. Cabin, is to give the child a positive attitude toward food. Educational psychologist Robert E. Calmes, Ed.D., professor emeritus of the University of Arizona in Tucson, agrees. Food has to be seen by the child for what it is: a way of showing genuine care and concern for the living body as well as a source of pleasure, says Dr. Calmes. "Limiting the quantities of that food is as much a way of showing care for the body as is serving food that tastes good."

How do you get your child to understand this concept? You talk to her as much as possible. Experts at Eating Disorders Awareness and Prevention in Seattle say that feelings of inadequacy or a lack of control in life are among the psychological factors that contribute to eating disorders. By helping your child to learn how she can control her food intake while enjoying that food and its positive effects on the way she feels and looks, you will increase her feelings of adequacy and control.

Take the lead. It's important for parents to model the behavior they want their kids to follow, says Dr. Calmes. By showing your child that you enjoy healthful amounts of food in your own life, you can teach her how to eat sensibly. Dr. Calmes's six-step plan in chapter 11 for having a happy, healthy family illustrates this concept in more detail.

Become a keen observer. Is your child making more mistakes lately? Is she having a bit more trouble remembering things? In general, has she shown a decreased interest in her social involvement? Does she seem to have less motor control? Has her activity level either decreased or increased dramatically? One 5-year-old girl began to run obsessively at school recess and after eating so she wouldn't get fat. Children who exercise compulsively may have a form of an eating disorder, even if their food intake seems normal.

Watch her when she eats. Is she playing with her food? Pretending to eat? Slipping food to the dog or into her pockets? She may also be skipping meals, especially breakfast. According to a study of children ages 9 to 11, serious eating problems can start just from not eating breakfast.

Practice healthy, active living. Make noncompetitive physical movement—running, walking, bicycling, dancing, gardening—a significant part of your family's life. Again, you'll get a better sense of how to integrate physical activity fun into your family's lifestyle with the help of Dr. Calmes's plan in chapter 11.

Discover food appreciation 101. Teach your child to appreciate fresh food. Tell her you've adopted nouvelle cuisine as a hobby you want to share with her. Take her to dinner at restaurants known for their lovely dishes or to other local places where healthful food is showcased, like farmers' markets or food festivals. Watch cooking demonstrations on television. Buy books about or, if possible, visit the food-loving regions of California, France, or Italy, where preparation of nutritious food is a way of life.

Share. Tell your child, in a communicative, nonsensational way, about the personal dangers of anorexia and bulimia. Share books with her that will help her understand how to avoid this terrible trap. *101 Ways to Help Your Daughter Love Her Body,* by Brenda Lane and Elaine Rehr, contains some ideas you are bound to find

The Dangerous High of Eating Disorders

Extreme dieting gets your daughter (or son) more than just thin. It gets her high—gloriously, energetically, but *dangerously* high in a way that is addictive and will mislead you into thinking she is healthy and happy and must be eating well. That can be a dangerous mistake.

After extended fasting (or severely limiting calorie and especially carbohydrate intake), her body begins burning fat and protein as alternative energy sources. Since no carbohydrate is present and because fat does not burn as completely and efficiently as carbohydrates do, the liver subsequently converts fat into usable compounds called ketone bodies.

Most cells can use ketone bodies for energy, but when more ketone bodies are produced than can be used, their levels rise in the blood, leading to a state called ketosis. Ketosis in itself is not life-threatening, but it can actually be a factor in death by starvation. How? It usually produces a mental state that is described as not only euphoric, but mentally alert, physically energetic, and lacking any feelings of hunger. When this happens, the person feels marvelous, performs well, and senses, correctly, that she will lose this sense of energized happiness by eating normally. Considering this sense of psychological mastery over the body's need for food, says Dr. Cabin, it becomes clear why people become addicted to their eating disorders. Not eating feels marvelous!

helpful. *Mom, I Feel Fat: Becoming Your Daughter's Ally in Developing Healthy Body Image,* by Sharon A. Hersh, provides a God-centered and faith-based orientation if that approach would be suitable for your family.

Unfortunately, at the same time that your child is feeling this incredible high, her body is suffering the destructive effects of her disorder. Mental as well as physical results of food deprivation are setting in. These symptoms can show up without her being consciously aware of them. Some examples of these symptoms include the following:

- Her behavior may become inappropriately mystical. She may begin feeling that she's in touch with spiritual forces that make her all the more sure that not eating is the right thing to do.
- She may become confused and tired at school and work. Eating is the last thing she is able to care about.
- Her fear of eating may be overriding her instinct to survive. She may be literally unable to eat, even if convinced by people who care about her that she must eat to live. If she doesn't eat for 10 to 14 days, she could die.

With so much pressure on kids to be thin, you need to be careful not to let your child diet on her own. Get involved with your child's diet from an early age—and stay involved, especially through the difficult preteen and teen years. Discuss what she's eating (or not eating), and work with her to get the right balance of nutrition that will enable her to stay at a comfortable weight. Show her with your own habits that eating well can be enjoyed all day, every day.

You might also want to log on to www.something-fishy.org. Dedicated to providing information about eating disorders, this Web site offers a list of books for all levels of eating disorders (from mild dissatisfaction with weight to near terminal bulima and anorexia) and ages, all of which have been reviewed. The www.Gurze.com site, recommended by Jeanne Rust, director of Mirasol, The Arizona Center for Eating Disorder Recovery, also has a great list of books. Finally, the National Eating Disorders Association Web site (www.NationalEatingDisorders.org) contains entire courses teaching children of all ages how to have healthy relationships with their bodies, eat for health, and avoid eating disorders. You might have your kids' schools or organizations (such as Girl Scouts) present these courses or get together with other parents and teach them yourselves.

Beware the euphoria. Especially be on the lookout for suddenly euphoric moods in your child. If she finds everything suddenly wonderful, loves everything you say and do, and seems to love being involved with the preparation of food more than ever before, watch out. She could be in the euphoria-inducing phase of an eating disorder, says Dr. Cabin.

Be cautious about diets. Seek help from your pediatrician if your child goes on—and stays on—any kind of diet. The Harvard Eating Disorders Center warns that "many eating disorders get their start from a simple diet or inadvertent weight loss." And don't kid yourself: Eating disorders do not just go away. Children do not outgrow them. When a person becomes the victim of an eating disorder, she develops an actual change in the way she perceives her body. No matter how cadaverous she seems to others, for instance, or how far her bones stick out, that body she sees in the mirror is still too fat to her, according to the Harvard center.

Find a specialist. If you do suspect that your child has the signs of an eating disorder, find a specialist in eating disorders as soon as possible. Your pediatrician should be able to refer you.

Know that help is available. If you suspect that your child has an eating disorder, there are some organizations that may be able to help you. The National Eating Disorders Association Web site referred to earlier (www.NationalEatingDisorders.org) has 24-hour-a-day referral services. Or call the National Association of Anorexia Nervosa and Associated Disorders at (847) 831-3438 for a referral to a treatment specialist, clinic, or support group in any of the 50 states. (You can also check out their Web site at www.anad.org.) Another likely source of help: your local library. Ask the information specialist or reference librarian for a list of eating disorder specialists in your town and call them to find out about services, price, and consultants who will talk to you by phone.

If you have health insurance, call the company and ask a consultant about the kind of coverage you have on eating disorders. Remember, eating disorder clinics and treatments can be very expensive. Make sure you know the cost before committing your child to any kind of care. Support group services are free; call Overeaters Anonymous (they're listed in the phone book) if your town has a chapter. Just don't give up no matter how often you are told by "experts" (including your family physician) that your child is probably fine and will get over her symptoms and/or that you cannot afford the kind of treatment your child really needs.

Food Allergies and Sensitivities

A food allergy is a measurable response by your child's body to a certain kind of food. Common allergens for children include milk, eggs, soy, peanuts, wheat, and citrus fruits. Common symptoms of food allergies include tingling of the lips, palate, tongue, or throat; hoarseness; nausea, vomiting, or diarrhea; hives, eczema, and itching; chest tightness and breathing problems; and nasal congestion, runny nose, and sneezing. A food sensitivity is generally not as serious as a measurable allergy, which can in some cases be fatal, but still causes your child discomfort with cramps, headaches, rashes, runny nose, or recurring infection.

In addition to these symptoms, a child's mood may change after he eats a food to which he is sensitive or allergic. Some foods can create inflammatory responses in a child's central nervous system that cause behavioral swings. What may look like severe anxiety in a child could turn out to be an allergy or sensitivity to foods, according to Dr. Cabin. It could also be a reaction to chemicals that cause certain odors in perfumes and other strong-smelling substances, such as cleaning products or gasoline.

In severe cases, a person may go into anaphylactic shock after being exposed to an allergen. This is a deadly condition that can result in widespread itching and welts, difficulty breathing, nausea, vomiting, and a drop in blood pressure that can cause the circulation of blood and oxygen to come to a halt. If the person doesn't get immediate medical treatment, this condition can be fatal. Anaphylaxis isn't always an instant reaction; it can take a few hours for symptoms to occur.

Beware a dramatic improvement in mood. Anaphylaxis can be characterized by a sudden improvement in mood, caused by the oxygen supply to the brain being cut off. If your child has any kind of dramatic upsurge in mood, such as an upswing of happiness, after eating a certain food, get him to an emergency room.

I know of a college woman who became giddy and euphoric an hour or so after eating a tropical fruit. She would have died had her alert fiancé not insisted she be checked by a doctor just in case. Her body had had such a severe allergic reaction to this fruit that it was already in a state of oxygen deprivation. By the time the emergency room physicians diagnosed this woman's condition, she was, she says, "on my way out—of this world." Luckily, they were able to treat her in time.

Get help fast. Watch for a sudden inability to breathe or talk or even move, which indicates the allergic reaction has sent the body into complete anaphylactic shock. If this occurs, call 911 or get your child to the emergency room immediately.

Banish the allergen. Once the offending food has been identified, make sure your child completely eliminates it from his diet. This includes even minute amounts where the offending food might be just one among many ingredients. No cheating can be allowed, ever.

Medical testing. The diagnosis of allergies remains a controversial topic among many doctors, and many practitioners of alternative medicine will use testing methods not accepted as valid by conventional doctors. Dr. Cabin suggests asking if your child's physician uses a blood test known as a radioallergosorbent test (RAST), which identifies the presence of several different antibodies. He also suggests inquiring about electrodermal testing and food elimination testing for food allergies. If the doctor seems unwilling to discuss these medical tests or suggests that such tests are probably unnecessary, this doctor may not be the best one for this situation, says Dr. Cabin.

Observation testing. Testing for food sensitivities is often done through the simple approach of an elimination diet. The foods that are suspected to be causing the sensitivity are eliminated from the diet for about 2 weeks, then reintroduced one at a time to measure their effect on your child.

Coping with allergies. If your child has a food allergy, make sure he is under a physician's care, and work with the doctor to create alternate eating plans that exclude all traces of the offending foods. Don't think this work is temporary: Food allergies don't usually go away.

Even the simple joys of traveling can become difficult when your child has food allergies. You may need to send permissible food ahead to your hotel so the chef can prepare it with your family's meals or learn to interrogate restaurant managers on the most minute details of their food preparation to make sure your child's meal does not include use of the forbidden foods. You might also need to avoid traveling to certain countries whose governments do not require listing all of a food's ingredients on the label.

Once you find out what foods your child is and is not allergic to, though, you can become creative about making his culinary experiences as delightful and nutritious as they possibly can be. By looking for alternative foods that your child can eat, you just might discover some delicious foods your entire family will enjoy.

basics of nutrition and planning your child's menu

To me, the real problem with the way we eat is that it's regarded as a recreational pastime. The fast-food industry has made what used to be "treat" foods, such as milkshakes and french fries, part of the everyday diet. Vending machines have made candy bars and sugared sodas acceptable food for any time of the day. Convenience stores have made the 32-ounce caffeinated soda the popular choice when you're thirsty, and coffee bars have made frothy sweet coffee, espresso, and cappuccino acceptable beverages to use as a reward, source of comfort, or quick pleasure at any hour. Children learn that indulging in these foods and drinks any time they want, in unlimited amounts, is an inalienable right.

What we've forgotten is that we need to monitor our food intake and, ideally, plan for it in advance. People in other cultures seem to know how to do this instinctively and limit their food con-

71

sumption to small portions at the primary meals and very light snacks in between. No eating in the car, no enormous bags of potato chips in front of the TV, no rushed meals of heavily processed foods.

In Italy, there is even a trend called the Slow-Food Movement, which teaches that only fresh food, properly grown and prepared, should be eaten. This movement supports its educational activities by publishing highly regarded guides for choosing, preparing, serving, and enjoying Italian food and wine.

No fast food? You must be joking!

In America, we go from fast-food restaurants to all-you-can-eat buffets and consider home-cooked meals any kind of processed food we can pop in the toaster or microwave oven.

There is, however, the inescapable fact that if we take in more calories than our bodies need, we will gain weight. Kids are no different. If they consistently go beyond their calorie budget, their health, appearance, and mood will suffer, and their risk for certain diseases, such as diabetes, obesity, and depression, may increase. Of the food we do eat, a large percentage must contain nutrients the body needs or we can become malnourished—a sad thought in this country of prosperity.

For this reason, it's essential that you very carefully monitor the calories from "unhealthful" foods (foods that do not nourish the body, such as refined sugar and refined flour) that you and, especially, your children consume. Not only do these foods fill up your child's body without nourishing it, they tend to cause cravings for even more unhealthful food. Once your child begins eating them, she'll want more and more of these foods—and less and less of the veggies, fruit, and lean protein that her body needs to thrive. It is interesting that the really nutritious foods (except for very starchy vegetables and sugar-filled fruits) are almost never addictive.

These cravings plague adults, but they're particularly devastating to children. Fortunately, there is hope. You can avoid getting your children "hooked" on high-calorie, unnourishing foods by giving them a healthy diet from their earliest years. And, even if they've already started this addiction, it's never too late to act to help them break free of it.

Finally, don't think that just because your older child can eat by herself, maybe even prepare her own simple meal, she no longer needs your guidance in making food choices. Your goal should be to make your children want, and enjoy, the foods they need most in order to look, feel, and act their best, in the quantities that are best for them. It's not always easy to do this, but there are some proven strategies to make this happen. You'll learn some of them below and find even more detailed information in chapters 9, 10, and 11.

The Basics of Food Planning

Reevaluating your child's diet doesn't need to be a complex, time-consuming task. To determine your child's calorie and protein needs for optimum development, simply take a look at the chart "How Much Food Should My Child Eat?" on page 74. When you're planning your child's diet, start with the proteins that you plan on serving, then deduct their calorie amounts from the day's allotment. (See "Calorie and Protein Content of Common Foods" on page 78 for a partial list.) Then you'll know how many calories can be allowed for other foods, such as carbohydrates and fats. If you follow these guidelines, your child should get her full supply of vitamins and minerals, and you should be able to keep your child's weight from escalating.

How Much Food Should My Child Eat?

Here is what an American child's diet should look like, based on age and, for older children, gender. (*Note:* The standard energy and protein needs in growing children are additionally assessed by height as well as by weight. The chart below reflects nutritional needs by weight only.)

Category	Age (Years)	Calories per Day	Protein per Day (g)
Children	1–3	1,300	16
	4–6	1,800	24
	7–10	2,000	28
Adolescent males	11–14	2,500	45
	15–18	3,000	59
Adolescent females	11–14	2,200	46
	15–18	2,200	44

Reprinted with permission from *Recommended Dietary Allowances*, 10th edition.
Copyright 1989 by the National Academy of Sciences. Courtesy of the National Academy Press, Washington, D.C.

A New Food Pyramid

The now famous USDA Food Pyramid was created about 10 years ago, based on the U.S. government's recommended daily allowances (RDAs) for key nutritional requirements. Yet while the RDAs have continued to be modified over the past 10 years, the pyramid has remained unchanged. As it stands today, in light of our new understanding of nutrition, the USDA Food Pyramid does not really promote the ideal diet, especially for children. Dr. Cabin's experience has shown that the USDA Food Pyramid places too much emphasis on complex carbohydrates and fruit and not enough on vegetables and protein, particularly red meat.

Dr. Cabin is not alone in his criticism of the USDA pyramid for menu planning. Walter Willett, M.D., chair of the department of nutrition at the Harvard School of Public Health, offers his own food pyramid, based on 2 decades of nutrition research. In his book *Eat, Drink, and Be Healthy*, Dr. Willett points out that the USDA has failed to distinguish between the "good" fats (like those in avocados, nuts, olives, and fish) and the "bad" fats (like those found in fried fast food and margarine). These bad fats, or trans fats, not only increase the level of "bad" cholesterol in your child's bloodstream, but make matters worse by actually decreasing the level of healthy cholesterol. He also points out that the USDA makes no distinction between different kinds of carbohydrates. Dr. Willett's pyramid corrects these problems by, among other changes, stressing the need for whole grain foods at most meals and the need to "use sparingly" the refined carbohydrates like white rice, white bread, potatoes, pasta, and sweets.

Dr. Cabin and I applaud Dr. Willett's innovations and believe they are a great leap forward, especially in helping parents plan their kids' menus. In order for parents to give their children the best nutrition possible, however, we would like to offer some revisions that we believe will result in even better behaved children for those who follow its dietary guidelines. We call this the Good Attitude Food Pyramid, and you can use it every day to help plan what you and your family will eat. It is displayed in detail in the illustration on page 76.

Because this pyramid summarizes the recommendations in the rest of the book, we suggest making a copy of it and hanging it on your refrigerator for an instant reference.

The Good Attitude Food Pyramid

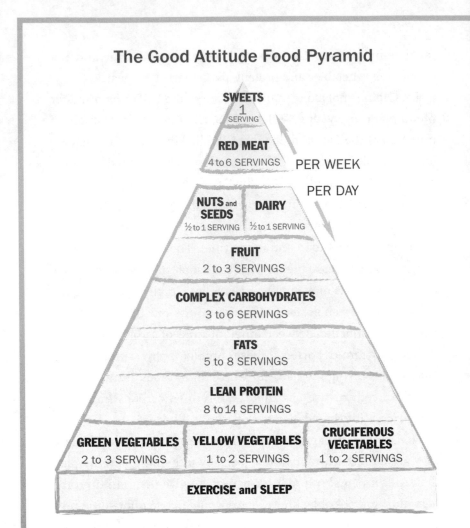

SWEETS
1 SERVING

RED MEAT
4 to 6 SERVINGS

PER WEEK

PER DAY

NUTS and SEEDS
½ to 1 SERVING

DAIRY
½ to 1 SERVING

FRUIT
2 to 3 SERVINGS

COMPLEX CARBOHYDRATES
3 to 6 SERVINGS

FATS
5 to 8 SERVINGS

LEAN PROTEIN
8 to 14 SERVINGS

GREEN VEGETABLES
2 to 3 SERVINGS

YELLOW VEGETABLES
1 to 2 SERVINGS

CRUCIFEROUS VEGETABLES
1 to 2 SERVINGS

EXERCISE and SLEEP

At the base of this plan is daily exercise and 9 hours of sleep per night. Vegetables and lean protein form the foundation. In addition to other green and yellow **vegetables**, your child should eat cruciferous vegetables, such as broccoli and cabbage. A serving of vegetables is 1 cup of raw leafy greens, ½ cup of other vegetables (cooked or chopped raw), or ¾ cup of vegetable juice. For the maximum range of nutrients, serve a variety of vegetables of different colors.

For **lean protein**, serve fowl, legumes, or fish at least three times a day. The fish should preferably be wild rather than farm-raised, and it should be small in size, such as salmon, mahi mahi, trout, haddock, catfish, or perch. Due to possible contamination, avoid larger fish such as tuna and swordfish. One serving of lean protein equals 1 ounce of cooked fish, shellfish, or fowl; one egg; or ½ cup of cooked beans. You can also serve soy as a source of protein once a day; a serving equals 1 cup.

For the **fats**, serve "good" fats such as olive oil, flaxseed oil, or canola oil. Avoid hydrogenated oils. A serving equals 1 teaspoon of oil or butter, 1 tablespoon of salad dressing or cream cheese, 5 large olives, 1 slice of bacon, or 2 tablespoons of sour cream.

Complex carbohydrates include whole grains and white potatoes. One serving equals one slice of whole wheat bread; half of a whole wheat bagel or muffin; ½ cup of cooked whole wheat grain cereal, whole wheat pasta, brown rice, or other whole grains; or ½ cup of corn, potatoes, or sweet potatoes.

A serving of **fruit** is equal to one small to medium piece of fresh fruit, ½ cup of canned or cut fruit, ¾ cup of fruit juice, ¼ cup of dried fruit, or 1 cup of berries or melon cubes. One of your child's daily servings of fruit should be an apple or an orange.

Seeds and nuts make great snacks; one serving is 1 ounce of shelled nuts or 2 tablespoons of nut butter.

A serving of **dairy** is equal to 1 ounce of hard cheese, 1 cup of milk or unsweetened yogurt, or ½ cup of ricotta or cottage cheese.

Red meat includes beef, lamb, pork, and wild game such as deer and elk. A serving equals 1 ounce of cooked meat. Note that children should be served red meat only two or three times per week, for a weekly total of about 6 ounces.

Sweets should be limited to less than one serving per week.

Calorie and Protein Content of Common Foods

For more listings and details, consult one of the suggested nutrition references on page 204.

Fruits	Amount	Calories	Protein (g)
Apple	1 medium	67	<1
Applesauce, unsweetened	1 cup	104	<1
Banana	1 medium	104	1
Grapefruit	½ large	37	<1
Grapes	17 small	69	<1
Kiwifruit	1 medium	61	1
Mangoes, cubed	1 cup	54	<1
Melon	1 cup	60	<1
Orange	1 small	84	<1
Peach	1 medium	56	<1
Pear	1 small	67	<1
Raisins	1 oz	84	<2
Raspberries	1 cup	60	<1
Strawberries, whole	1¼ cups	54	<1
Watermelon, cubed	1¼ cups	64	<1

Vegetables	Amount	Calories	Protein (g)
Asparagus, spears	6	25	3
Baked potato, with skin	1 small (3 oz)	80	3
Broccoli, chopped, cooked	1 cup	45	5
Cabbage, shredded, raw	1 cup	25	1
Carrots, sliced, cooked	1 cup	70	2
Celery, sticks, raw	1 cup	20	1
Corn kernels	½ cup	89	3

Vegetables	Amount	Calories	Protein (g)
Green beans, cooked	½ cup	22	1
Green peas, cooked	½ cup	80	4
Lettuce, loose leaf, large	2 leaves	10	<1
Mixed green salad	1 cup	25	<1
Spinach, cooked, drained	½ cup	21	3
Squash, butternut, baked	½ cup	68	1
Tomato, sliced	1 cup	38	2
Vegetable juice	¾ cup	45	2
Zucchini	½ cup	22	1

Eggs, Cheese, and Dairy Products	Amount	Calories	Protein (g)
Butter	1 tsp	45	0
Cheese, low-fat (all types)	1 oz	50	7
Cottage cheese, low-fat	½ cup	80	14
Cream cheese, nonfat	2 Tbsp	28	4
Cream cheese, reduced-fat	2 Tbsp	45	5
Egg, large	1	75	6
Egg substitute, liquid	¼ cup	55	7
Egg white	1	17	4
Milk, nonfat, vitamin A added	1 cup	86	8
Milk, 1% low-fat	1 cup	102	8
Milk, soy	1 cup	80	7
Milk, whole	1 cup	150	8
Sour cream, low-fat	2 Tbsp	40	2
Sour cream, nonfat	2 Tbsp	31	2
Yogurt, nonfat fruit	1 cup	232	10

(continued)

Breads, Cereals, and Grains	Amount	Calories	Protein (g)
Bagel, small	½	80	3
Bran flake cereal	¾ cup	114	3
Bread, multigrain	1 slice	69	3
Bread, oat	1 slice	67	2
Bread, rye	1 slice	65	2
Bread, whole wheat	1 slice	70	3
Cornbread	1 slice (about 2½ oz)	161	4
Couscous, cooked	1 cup	68	2
Cream of rice, cooked	1 cup	126	4
Cream of wheat, cooked	1 cup	131	4
English muffin	1	160	6
Millet, cooked	½ cup	143	4
Oatmeal, cooked	1 cup	145	6
Pasta, rotini, cooked	1 cup	197	7
Pita bread	½	75	3
Quinoa, dry	¼ cup	160	6
Rice, brown or white, cooked	⅓ cup	80	3

Meat, Poultry, and Fish	Amount	Calories	Protein (g)
Beef, round, lean, roasted	1 oz	40	7
Catfish, cooked	1 oz	40	6
Chicken breast, skinless, cooked	1 oz	30	7
Halibut, baked	1 oz	40	7
Pork tenderloin, lean, roasted	1 oz	53	7
Roast beef, lean, cooked	1 oz	33	7
Salmon, baked	1 oz	52	7

Meat, Poultry, and Fish	Amount	Calories	Protein (g)
Salmon, smoked	1 oz	33	6
Sea bass, cooked	1 oz	42	7
Shrimp, steamed	1 oz	28	6
Sole, steamed	1 oz	32	7
Tuna, in water	1oz	35	7
Turkey breast, skinless, cooked	1 oz	35	7

Miscellaneous Foods	Amount	Calories	Protein (g)
Balsamic vinegar	1 Tbsp	13	0
Cookie, oatmeal	1 average	80	1
Granola bar	1 small	120	2
Jams or preserves	1 Tbsp	50	<1
Mayonnaise, reduced-fat	1 Tbsp	45	0
Oil	1 Tbsp	110	0
Peanut butter, reduced-fat	2 Tbsp	190	14
Popcorn	3 cups	71	2
Pudding, prepared, no sugar	½ cup	90	5
Ranch dressing, nonfat	1 Tbsp	17	1
Salsa	¼ cup	20	1
Seeds, sunflower	¼ cup	205	8
Soup, bean, vegetarian canned	1 cup	130	7
Soup, vegetable	1 cup	80	2
Spaghetti sauce, plain	½ cup	94	2
Vinaigrette dressing	1 Tbsp	6	0
Walnuts	1 oz	180	4
Yogurt bar, frozen, nonfat	½ cup	100	4

Guidelines for Meals and Snacks

Here are some more important things to keep in mind when choosing your meal plans and snacking strategies.

Serving Proteins to Kids

Foods containing all of the essential amino acids that your child's body requires are called complete proteins and come almost exclusively from animal products such as eggs, milk, meat, and fish. Many of the amino acids found in animal products are naturally antidepressant in nature, especially in the combinations found in meat. Also, complete proteins are important for building a healthy nervous system and brain and keeping them in good, nonfrazzled repair. (Nerves can become frayed just like fibers in fabric, causing irritability and lots of other unwanted feelings.)

The only plant source of complete proteins is soy, which should be served in moderation to kids (no more than one meal per day). Vegetables, grains, and beans lack one or more of the essential amino acids and so are called incomplete proteins. For optimum health, these foods should not be relied upon entirely for your child's daily protein needs or should at least be combined with other proteins (red beans paired with rice, for instance). Dr. Cabin emphasizes that his food pyramid is meant to be a minimum basic guide. A few more servings of certain foods per day than those listed in the pyramid (except for soy, sweets, and red meat) won't hurt and can only help your child's good attitude grow and develop.

Food really is fuel for the body, and as such, it should be dispensed in regular amounts. While prehistoric people would feast for days on a "kill" and then go for days without eating till the next hunting-party success, the human body is much happier and more productive when we eat in regular amounts at regular times throughout the day. This keeps hunger from getting too intense (as every mom knows, there is no stronger cause of rudeness and bad attitude than basic hunger from not having eaten). Your child's three meals should all be roughly the same size, containing approximately the same amount of protein and calories.

Serving Fats to Kids

Contrary to what many diet books would have you believe, your child needs fats in his diet. As the parent, it is your job to distinguish between health-promoting types of fats and potentially

The Impact of Sleep on Kids' Rudeness

Getting enough sleep is almost as important for curing kids' rudeness as making sure they're eating a healthful diet. According to the National Institutes of Health (NIH), research shows that children from ages 7 to 11 who get 9 hours of sleep every night:

- Have better moods
- Perform better in school
- Suffer fewer accidents
- Are less likely to be obese
- Show fewer signs of Attention Deficit Hyperactivity Disorder (ADHD) or Attention Deficit Disorder (ADD)
- Have better attendance in school

To take advantage of the positive effects of a good night's sleep, make sure your elementary-school-age kids are in bed by 8:00 P.M., recommends the NIH. And don't let your adolescents become regular viewers of Jay Leno or David Letterman. Determine an appropriate bedtime for your teens, and strictly enforce it. Finally, tell a friend. Start a campaign to make other parents and teachers aware that children need 9 hours of sleep a night.

The Impact of Exercise on Kids' Rudeness

Children who are physically active are less likely to feel bad and, therefore, less likely to behave rudely. Exercise can improve mood in several ways. Studies have shown that exercise not only can reduce but also can prevent depression. Regular workouts also help children—as well as adults—deal with stressful events by enabling them to relieve some anxiety and helping them clear their minds. Further, exercise increases the body's production of mood-lifting beta endorphins.

Even more promising, research has shown that kids who exercise are less likely to be overweight than those who don't exercise, and they're more interested in learning. As an added bonus, children who exercise are more likely to get the sleep their bodies require because they sleep more deeply.

harmful varieties. The seeds, nuts, and fish in the Lean Protein Level of the Good Attitude Food Pyramid provide all the health-promoting omega-3 fatty acids your child should need. For an extra boost of omega-3s, you might choose to give your child flaxseed oil, which is a great substitute for butter, or salad dressings made from cold-pressed vegetable oils. Your child should consume saturated fats only in complete protein foods, such as meat and eggs.

Fats used as salad dressings or food toppings should be unsaturated oils from plants and nuts. Hydrogenated oils are former unsaturated oils, such as corn or canola oil, that have been processed with hydrogen, rendering them more solid at room temperature. The more solid an oil, the longer its shelf life. The longer shelf life may be good for food corporations and supermarket merchants, but it's not good for your child. The more solid an oil is, the more saturated—and thus more harmful to your child's health—it is.

In addition, the harder and more solid an oil is, the more trans fatty acids it is likely to contain. As new research is being done, scientists are discovering more and more harmful effects of a diet high in trans fatty acids. For instance, the consumption of trans fatty acids is related to increased levels of LDL ("bad") cholesterol in the blood, which is associated with an increased possibility of coronary heart disease. Allowing your child to eat as much of the foods that contain trans fatty acids as he wants sets him up for coronary heart disease later on—which is the number one cause of death in the United States.

There is also reason to suspect that trans fatty acids can harm your child's good attitude and mood, says Dr. Cabin. As mentioned earlier in this book, studies have shown that children with poor behavior and symptoms of Attention Deficit Hyperactivity Disorder (ADHD) have low levels of omega-3 fatty acids, which are so important to good brain health. Due to their molecular shape, Dr. Cabin theorizes, the trans fatty acids might hinder the absorption of omega-3 fatty acids—in the event the child were getting any of these good fats in his diet, that is. "But it's my suspicion that parents who allow their kids to eat large amounts of food that contains trans fatty acids are not going to be concerned with making sure their kids get flaxseed and salmon and other foods containing the omega-3s," he says.

Saturated fat supplies the body with energy but also plays a major role in determining the amount of cholesterol in the body. Foods that are high in saturated fat should be eaten sparingly because they raise the risk of heart attack. Which is worse for the body: saturated fats or trans fatty acids? According to Dr. Cabin, trans fatty acids are probably worse for everyone. The body does

(continued on page 88)

DR. CABIN'S
Nutritional Breakthroughs

Why Does My Tummy Hurt?:
Martina's Story

Martina is a lovely, vibrant 13-year-old girl, the only daughter of parents who dote on her and have provided her with the best tutoring they can find in academic and enrichment subjects. Her mother, who has a Ph.D. in physics, has put her career on hold so she can raise Martina, and her father has made a career in consulting from his home so he can be with his beloved family as much as possible.

Though bright, eager to learn, and very outgoing, Martina was not as happy as her parents would have liked. For years, she had had a tendency to be easily upset. She also tended to overreact in emotional situations and to go into melancholy moods. Yet she held her feelings inside, refusing to discuss what was bothering her. She also complained of abdominal pain and loss of appetite but showed no weight loss.

A gastroenterologist Martina's parents consulted was unable to help. His tests showed nothing wrong with her digestive system that would have caused the pain and loss of appetite.

When Martina came to see Dr. Cabin, he took a detailed medical history. From her history, Dr. Cabin suspected food sensitivities or allergies could be at work. To test this theory, he gave Martina a radioallergosorbent test (RAST), a blood test that can identify the presence of several different antibodies. The results showed that Martina was sensitive to fish, peanuts, dairy foods, sugar, and wheat. Elimination of these foods helped improve her mood dramatically, but not her abdominal pain.

The next step Dr. Cabin took was to eliminate all fried foods and sugar from Martina's diet. After more testing, he prescribed homeopathic remedies and his own brand of vitamins, including Mighty Multi, Really Serious C, and a calcium-based formula called Bone Jour, all in dosages proper for children. He also prescribed two types of digestive enzymes, Digease and Betaine HCL (hydrochloric acid).

Martina is now free of all troublesome symptoms and doing very well. Her mood has improved, and she is much better able to deal with her emotions. She now handles difficult situations more calmly, and she no longer has abdominal pain. Both she and her parents are thrilled with the results of Dr. Cabin's recommendations.

not recognize these fats as toxic and tries to absorb and use them just like nature-made fats. The effects on children's growing bodies and brains is unknown, but experts are beginning to suspect those effects will not be good, warns Dr. Cabin.

The trick is to get your child to learn to love the healthful oils, such as flaxseed oil and olive oil. Buy them in their nonhydrogenated forms. (Make sure the labels do not say "partially hydrogenated" or "hydrogenated.") In any vegetable oil, try to get brands that have been cold pressed, because heating oils destroys the omega-3 fatty acids. In the case of flaxseed oil, make sure the product you buy is kept refrigerated in the store. All vegetable oils should be kept refrigerated after being opened. One easy way to get your child used to eating olive oil instead of butter is to pour it in little dishes into which she can dip her bread. Lots of upscale restaurants have been using this method for years.

Finally, if you buy snacks with nonhydrogenated oils in them, such as special brands of chips or tortillas, pay close attention to the expiration date. These products have a shorter shelf life than the national brands of chips that use hydrogenated oils. You may have better luck buying them at a natural foods retailer that would be expected to have higher turnover in these items.

Serving Carbohydrates and Snacks to Kids

The rest of your child's diet should be composed mostly of complex carbohydrates. The most common sources include grains and legumes along with vegetables, nuts, seeds, fruits, and sea vegetables.

According to the Good Attitude Food Pyramid, your child should eat four to seven servings of vegetables of different colors a day, plus a serving or two of potato, brown rice, or corn. The best fruits to serve your child are apples and oranges, with constipation-easing fruits such as figs and prunes added as needed. Berries can be added in place of cakes and cookies.

Remember, refined white flour does not count as a complex carbohydrate even though it originated with grains. By removing all the "brown" components of the grain and bleaching the rest, the food business people created a product that has been wonderful for pastries, soft white breads, and cookies, but that is lacking in any nutrition whatsoever except for those vitamins added back in so that the flour can be called enriched. Avoid bread that is made with white flour whenever you can. The other varieties, such as whole wheat, rye, and pumpernickel, are much more delicious, anyway.

?? ASK DR. CABIN ??????????

Q. *Does my child need to take vitamin supplements?*

A. Yes, unless your child has an absolutely phenomenal diet of moderate portions of lean protein and fruit, vegetables, and whole grains grown organically in soil optimally rich in life-giving minerals. Your child's diet also needs to be free of nutrient-stealing, empty-calorie-containing substances such as sugar, processed food, artificial colors and flavors, preservatives, fast foods, caffeine, fatty foods, and fried foods.

Generally, I recommend a high-quality multiple vitamin and mineral supplement, a high-quality calcium supplement, and a source of omega-3 fatty acids (fish oil or flax). Many children require an additional strong antioxidant supplement—especially in the event of exposure to chemicals and low-quality food. In addition, individualized, specific nutrients may be recommended for the child, depending on his or her needs.

Serving Beverages to Kids

Beverages should be water, first and foremost. Dr. Cabin recommends 8 to 12 ounces of mineral or filtered tap water about every 2 hours. Stevia-sweetened herbal teas, hot or iced, are okay for treats. Once all other sugar sources have been removed from your child's diet, you can gradually add back in some 100 percent fruit juices. Calcium-fortified juices (preferably organic) can be given on special occasions or when an illness seems to have settled in.

6

the best and worst attitude-altering foods for your child

Let's face it. With all the hustle and bustle of running a household and perhaps working outside the home, you probably don't have the time to be a nutritionist and study the effects of every food on your child's health and emotions. But you still want to give him the best diet you can. You just need it to be easy to understand and easy to put into practice.

With that in mind, here are two short lists of the foods that most deserve your attention. The first list details the best foods and supplements to get into your child's diet; the second list notes the most harmful foods that you should try to avoid.

Adding the healthful foods into your child's diet and subtracting the offending ones is the best defense against your child developing food-related behavioral problems.

Good Attitude Foods

The following foods are the most powerful dietary weapons available to boost your child's feelings of cheerfulness and balance and give her a sense of well-being.

Take advantage of nature's mood lifters. "In some cases, omega-3 fatty acids can do as much for a child's emotional well-being as antidepressant and Ritalin-type drugs—without the side effects," says Dr. Cabin. That's because omega-3 fatty acids have anti-inflammatory, immune-stimulating, and mood-enhancing effects on children. The best sources are fish oil and flaxseed oil, or combinations of these oils.

Dr. Cabin recommends the following daily dosages—for children ages 12 and above: two capsules of fish oil or flaxseed oil, or 1 tablespoon of flaxseed oil; ages 6 to 12: one capsule of fish oil or flaxseed oil, or ½ tablespoon of flaxseed oil; infants and children up to 6 years old: ½ capsule of fish oil or flaxseed oil, or ¼ tablespoon of flaxseed oil. (In addition, if they're not being breastfed, infants should be given a formula that is supplemented with DHA and omega-6 fatty acids.) A capsule contains 1,000 milligrams, or half a tablespoon, of oil.

Start incorporating the oil into your child's diet slowly, since too much too soon can cause digestive discomfort. Cheaper yet is sprinkling 1 tablespoon of fresh ground flaxseed onto your child's food. Dr. Cabin recommends that all parents give their children these additional fatty acids. (The only exception is Eskimos, who get enough through their regular diet.)

If you purchase omega-3s in supplement form, make sure they are cold or expeller pressed (not hydrogenated). Refrigerate oils, seeds, and capsules after opening to keep them from becoming rancid.

You can expect your child's feelings of well-being to be enhanced by the omega-3s in about 6 weeks, according to Dr. Cabin.

Sip some soothing water. The late Adele Davis, author of the classic *Let's Have Healthy Children*, was one of the first nutritionists to proclaim water to be nature's great nerve-soother. She explained that water maintains the vitality of the nerves by keeping them lubricated and in good health. Dr. Cabin concurs completely.

Children should consistently be given water in place of soda or flavored beverages. Dr. Cabin recommends giving your child one 8-ounce glass of water at least every 2 hours. To keep your child interested in drinking lots of water, buy mineral or drinking water by the case. Keep it in the refrigerator in the summer; serve it at room temperature or heated with a slice of lemon in the cooler seasons.

Call on calcium. Foods rich in calcium are extremely important because calcium not only builds strong bones but also provides important nutrition for the nervous system, notes Dr. Cabin. Plain organic yogurt is a marvelous source of calcium, as is plain kefir, a yogurtlike drink made of milk. Both contain live cultures that have already partially digested the milk product for the body. Another good source of calcium for children who can tolerate high-carbohydrate foods is calcium-fortified organic orange juice.

Be aware that cow's milk in any form is a common allergen for children. Not only can it be difficult to digest, but, unless it is organic, it can be loaded with pesticides, steroids, and other chemicals. If you notice that your child suffers from bloating, gas, belching, diarrhea, abdominal pain, or constipation when he consumes milk or cheese, he may have a lactose intolerance. Have him stop consuming milk and take him to his pediatrician as soon as possible, advises Dr. Cabin. He may be able to have milk prodre if he takes lactase tablets.

ld is not lactose intolerant, feel free to give him

jor source of calcium and complete protein—as long

as   ganic. Warm milk has an even stronger calming effect than cold milk, says Dr. Cabin, because the amino acid tryptophan (the "feel good" amino acid) is more easily absorbed by the body from warm milk than from cold.

Dr. Cabin warns against giving calcium in the form of dolomite supplements because they are likely to contain lead. Likewise, avoid calcium carbonate, which is actually chalk and is a bit hard for the body to absorb. If you need to give your child calcium supplements, stick to calcium citrate, which is more easily absorbed.

Go nuts for calcium, too. If your child isn't able to enjoy dairy products, try giving him organic sunflower seeds, raw or toasted without salt, which are also a great natural source of calcium. Other excellent sources include almonds and almond milk, sesame seeds, almond butter, tahini (sesame seed butter), and green leafy vegetables such as chard, collards, kale, cooked beet greens, mustard greens, and (cooked or raw) turnip greens. Other terrific calcium builders include broccoli, kidney beans, okra, parsnips, parsley, and raw watercress.

If your child is a particularly adventurous eater, try cooked or raw sea vegetables, especially hijiki, kelp, and wakame. You can buy these nicely packaged in the health food store, complete with instructions for preparation. Sea vegetables are a staple food in the Asian diet, and they will become delicious to your children as well. Many varieties come all chopped up in handy shakers, often in combination with other calcium-rich foods such as sesame seeds.

Fill your child with fiber. Foods that are high in fiber are important for ending rudeness because they help prevent constipation. The American Gastroenterology Association states that a "main cause" of constipation can be a diet "high in animal fats . . . and refined sugar . . . but low in fiber." Further, studies suggest that high-fiber diets result in larger stools, more frequent bowel movements, and, therefore, less constipation. Dr. Cabin agrees and warns that it's not enough to buy processed foods with labels proclaiming "fiber added." The most valuable fiber is natural fiber, the kind found in raw or lightly cooked whole grains, fruits, and vegetables.

A good fiber supplement is natural psyllium, says Dr. Cabin— not the commercial kind that has been adulterated with dyes, sugar, or artificial sweeteners. You can buy natural psyllium in bulk in health food stores in the form of husks, seeds, or powder. A teaspoon added to food or drinks three times a day will greatly improve your child's regularity. Always accompany psyllium doses with a glass of water, and never serve more than a teaspoon of psyllium at a time. In portion sizes larger than a teaspoon, this powerful fiber can create bulking in the intestinal tract leading to bloating, gas, cramps, and pain.

Teach your kids that vegetables are not vile! In addition to being a source of calcium, vegetables such as broccoli, green beans, parsley, spinach, and dark green lettuces (not iceberg) contain the B-vitamins and minerals that are so important for a child's sense of well-being. Some of these vitamins are the precursors for the amino acids that serve as nature's antidepressants. One example is B_6, which is the precursor to tryptophan. Several medical studies have associated a lack of B vitamins, especially folate and B_{12}, with depression.

The vegetables you feed your family need to be organic—grown without pesticides. Buy them in a store that sells organic produce, or try growing your own. Don't worry about not having enough land for a garden; many vegetables grow in small plots of land or even in containers. Consult one of the many resources available on this subject; see page 205 for suggested reading.

Buy some confetti-colored veggies. Bright red peppers! Neon-yellow squash! Creamy off-white cauliflower! Scarlet radishes! Purple onions! Giving your child a colorful variety of vegetables serves as insurance that he is getting a good supply of B-vitamins, immune-strengthening antioxidants—vitamins C, E, and beta-carotene—and selenium and zinc as well as other minerals.

Learn to love legumes. Beans that are richly colored are loaded with minerals and fiber. Try red, black, and brown beans, all organically grown. Lentils are especially rich in mood-enhancing zinc. The paler-colored, starchy beans (such as northern, navy, and lima beans) are a bit less nutritious, but they're good occasionally for a tummy-filling change of pace and as a source of fiber.

While rich in protein, beans are not a source of complete proteins of the kind found in meat, fish, eggs, and milk. For this reason, Dr. Cabin does not recommend relying on them for your child's entire protein requirement.

Strengthen immunity with fruit. Because all types of fruit are rich sources of antioxidants and natural fiber, they are important for strengthening the immune system and promoting regularity. A strong immune system is more likely to ward off infections and illness that make the child feel awful and behave rudely. Fewer bouts with illness also means that your child needs fewer of the mood-clouding antibiotics that so often cause a bad attitude.

Fruits that contain high amounts of sugar, such as watermelon, grapes, and plums, should be eaten in moderation (probably in 1-ounce servings per day or not at all if your child has rudeness problems and carb-cravings after eating just a few carbohydrates). Kids should eat at least one apple every day. Fruits containing lower amounts of carbs, such as citrus fruits, cantaloupe, and honeydew, can be served in larger amounts.

Bring on the berries. Blueberries contain immune-enhancing nutrients in very large amounts; strawberries and raspberries are also terrific immune system builders. All berries are very high in fiber. It's especially important that you look for organic berries; because of their small size and closeness to the soil, berries tend to have more pesticide residue than other fruits. But all fruits mentioned here should be organically grown. The good news is that frozen organic berries can be purchased in most supermarkets these days and have virtually the same nutritional value as fresh-picked berries.

Go on a spree with sprouts and other superfoods. Broccoli sprouts, garlic, and wheat grass are examples of foods that contain enormous amounts of nutrients. Broccoli sprouts contain 20 to 30 times the healing benefits—including beta-carotene, vitamin C, and cancer-fighting phytochemicals called indoles—of the mature vegetable. Garlic contains organic sulfur compounds and phytochemicals that contribute to health and prevention of disease. Wheat grass contains blood-building chlorophyll, folate, vitamin B_6, and beta-carotene. Just a few ounces of these superfoods provide enormous benefits. Because they do so much to improve children's overall health, they are powerful emotional-health enhancers as well.

Be pro-protein (complete protein, that is). Meals containing complete proteins—the sort that are found in eggs, dairy foods, meat, and fish—can produce particularly dramatic mood changes in children. Protein is essential for growth and development as well as numerous other basic biological functions. Without it, children can feel weak, whiny, mentally confused, and out of sorts. Red meat supplies important natural combinations of iron and protein and can provide a natural "high." If you're worried about its saturated fat content, serve red meat only two times a week and make one portion just 3 ounces.

The meat you serve your family should come from chicken and beef that are raised without antibiotics and hormones. The fish should be wild fish, such as Alaskan salmon, mahi mahi, and Pacific cod, since farm-raised fish are treated with antibiotics. Stick to smaller fish, since the bigger the fish (such as tuna, swordfish, and sea bass), the more mercury it is likely to contain. Please avoid giving your child commercial hot dogs and breaded meats. The chemicals and preservatives in these products, such as nitrites and food dyes, can be nerve-wracking, literally, not to mention harmful in other ways.

Egg on those eggs. Dr. Cabin recommends eggs from free-range, organically fed chickens. This will be clearly marked on the box. Just be sure to use them in moderation: Limit your child's consumption of egg yolks to no more than four per week, suggests Dr. Cabin.

Nosh on nuts—with caution. The almond is considered to be a great tranquilizer, due to the high amount of magnesium (one of nature's most potent soothing minerals) and other mood-improving minerals it contains. Cashews, Brazil nuts, hazelnuts, and pecans are also high in magnesium.

Peanuts can be dangerous for a number of reasons. Peanuts and other stored nuts may harbor molds. They may contain aflatoxins, potent naturally carcinogenic substances caused by molds that cannot be boiled or roasted away. Most seriously, peanuts are a common allergen. In people with severe allergies, eating peanuts can lead to anaphylactic shock, an often severe and sometimes fatal reaction. I knew a little boy who had such a severe reaction to peanut butter that he had to be rushed to the emergency room and given adrenaline straight into his heart. Peanut allergies can develop at any time in a child's life, not just on the first taste.

Instead of peanut butter, serve your kids butters made with other kinds of nuts. You can buy almond and cashew and sometimes hazelnut butter in health food stores. Avoid commercial nut butters made with sugar and hydrogenated oils. Organic nuts are, of course, the best to buy. If you find them expensive, chop them up and serve them on fruit or casseroles or other dishes to make them go further.

Serve seeds for snacks. Pumpkin seeds are full of zinc, which is known to enhance mood and brain function. And, as mentioned earlier, sunflower seeds are loaded with calcium as well as magnesium.

Bad Attitude Foods

These foods are the hidden culprits that could be causing your child to act inappropriately. Surprisingly, some of these foods are commonly thought of as okay for kids. Happily, there are some great substitutes for the offending foods that your child will learn to enjoy just as much.

Foods with hidden sugar. Let's look at a typical American child's diet throughout a day.

Breakfast in a busy household might be a cereal bar with milk or perhaps a dish of cereal in fancy colors with favorite TV characters on the box and lots of fun things to read. Lunch could be a peanut butter or baloney sandwich on white bread. Dinner might

(continued on page 102)

DR. CABIN'S
Nutritional Breakthroughs

Walking Her Way to Better Grades, Better Behavior, and Better Health:

Selah's Story

It's hard to believe when you look at her, but sweet, curly-haired, pleasantly plump 6-year-old Selah was an intimidating bully of younger children. A moody, irritable child at school, she was not doing well academically and was unable to get along with her teacher. One activity she was good at was eating, and she would gorge on certain favorite foods. These were mostly white foods, such as mashed potatoes and chips and milk and especially ice cream. She had been eating this way for most of her life.

Her mother and father thought nothing of Selah's excess weight or unhealthy eating habits because they had always been big eaters who were overweight themselves. Besides eating, they were also fond of reading and film-watching and concert-going and many other cultural activities, all of which were sedentary in nature. Their one bad habit, they said, was smoking, but they decided everyone had to have one serious vice and smoking was such an enjoyable one.

One thing her parents weren't willing to ignore, however, was Selah's unpleasant disposition. Despite all attempts to change her behavior, including psychotherapy, Selah's parents could not change her bullying or bad moods or problems getting along with others. They worried that she would have these problems her entire life and also feared this hostile behavior could be a sign of an underlying medical problem. At that point, in an urgent search for answers, they consulted Dr. Cabin.

After running some routine medical tests, Dr. Cabin put the whole family on a diet that eliminated sugar and refined carbohydrates. He gave them strict orders to avoid sugary foods and beverages, white flour, artificial colors and flavors, and processed foods. The parents were also given homeopathic treatments that helped them give up smoking.

Dr. Cabin also encouraged the entire family to add more physical activity into their daily lives. They began taking walks every night after dinner and every afternoon during weekends. Selah's parents registered her in cheerleading, which she loved, and also put her on a soccer team, which boosted her activity level and helped her learn how to get along with other children.

After 3 months of these prescribed changes in lifestyle, the family was noticeably trimmer and happier. Selah had developed a happy social life and improved her grades at school. She was also getting praise from her teacher instead of blame. The bullying had stopped, and she was now getting along with other kids in a much more friendly manner.

be a quick, kid-pleasing casserole made with canned western-style beans and cut-up hotdogs. Or maybe it's that childhood favorite: slices of pepperoni pizza, bought frozen. The pizza might be accompanied by some frozen french fries or a frozen cheese-covered potato side dish. After-school and evening snacks could be toaster tarts, crackers with peanut butter, or tiny cheese-flavored crackers shaped like fish.

All the foregoing are favorite foods of children, found in any supermarket. Their packages feature well-known brand names belonging to famous national food companies. Not much sugar in any of these products, right?

Wrong. Look at the labels. All have sugar listed prominently on the ingredients list, either under the name "sugar" or some of the other names sugar goes by, such as dextrose and fructose. (See "Sweeteners Explained" on page 104 for more information on different types of sweeteners.) Since ingredients are listed in order of quantity, with the largest amount listed first, the closer to the top that sugar is listed, the more sugar the product contains.

By the end of the day, a child who eats foods such as those described above may have had enough sugar to turn his attitude for the worse. And he may well have snuck in other obviously sugar-rich foods like ice cream and gum. Can a parent find all of these favorite foods in products not containing sugar? In most cases, yes. Your best bet is to explore your supermarket's organic or health food sections. You can also find sugarless versions of these foods in natural foods supermarkets and many health food stores.

The dangers of soy. For adults, soy is considered a great substitute for meat and other animal foods that are sources of complete protein. But soy can present problems for children because it's a common allergen. Also, some studies have suggested that high soy consumption may actually lower IQ, presumably due to the processing of soy with glutamic acid, which is a neurotoxin.

Soy can also be difficult to digest. Dr. Cabin asserts that "ancient Chinese wisdom" suggested that the only kinds of soy that should be consumed by humans are fermented soy products (such as tempeh and soy sauce), while nonfermented soy products should be reserved for consumption by animals. He suggests limiting children's consumption of soy to 3 to 4 ounces a day. Tempeh is terrific because it can be packed for lunch and eaten straight from the package. The only real substitute containing as much complete protein as soy is, of course, an animal product, such as a hard-boiled egg or glass of milk or piece of meat.

The false promise of caffeine. A cup of hot chocolate, glass of iced tea, or can of caffeinated soda is regarded by many people to be a harmless spirit-lifter for children. True, caffeine may provide temporary energy and can have the paradoxical effect of calming a hyper child. But caffeine-containing beverages can also let the child down with a big drop in spirits and loss of feelings of well-being an hour or so after they're consumed. More caffeine is usually sought at that point, perpetuating a stimulant cycle that can make the child so edgy after a while that he feels out of control and unable to concentrate on any activity for more than a few minutes or so.

Herbal tea is a far better drink for kids, served hot or cold. Smoothies made with organic plain yogurt and fresh or frozen organic blueberries or pineapple or strawberries, sweetened with stevia, are also much healthier "refresher" drinks for kids than caffeinated drinks. (Stevia is a noncaloric sweetener that comes from the leaves of a South American shrub and is up to 300 times sweeter than sugar.)

(continued on page 108)

Sweeteners Explained

It's important that you, as a parent, understand how both natural and artificial sweeteners act in your child's body.

Nature's Sweeteners

Sugars are carbohydrates in various forms ranging from simple to complex. Two of the most common simple sugars are glucose, which is sometimes labeled as dextrose in processed foods, and fructose, found in fruits and honey.

More complex sugars include sucrose, found in common table sugar, maple syrup, and beet sugar; lactose, the principal carbohydrate of milk; and maltose, found in malt sugar and some cereal grains that have fermented.

Depending on how the sugar molecules are joined, they can form into either starch or fiber. Starches are found in such foods as grains, beans, and potatoes. In addition, glycogen, a form of starch, is found in meat, fish, and shellfish. Dextrin, which is made by breaking down starch, is found in processed foods and thickening agents. Fiber is found in fruits, vegetables, grains, nuts, and seeds.

Effects of Natural Sweeteners

When your child eats simple sugars, he absorbs them quickly, with little digestion. This causes his blood sugar levels to shoot up and his pancreas to secrete a huge amount of insulin to prevent the blood sugar from going too high. But alas, all of that insulin makes the blood sugar fall too low. The result can be a rush of adrenaline that can contribute to the rude feelings caused by the sudden drop in blood sugar, says Dr. Cabin. Because complex carbs are more slowly absorbed and digested by the body, they don't usually produce this response unless the child has a sugar metabolism problem.

Sugar Alcohols

Three sugar alcohols are currently available in the United States: mannitol, sorbitol, and xylitol. The sugar alcohols have as many calories as sugar but are absorbed so slowly that they don't cause the insulin and blood sugar level surges that regular sugars cause. However, they can cause terrible tummy trouble!

Because they are absorbed so slowly, the sugar alcohols remain in the bowel longer than natural sugars do, attracting even more digestive bacteria. The convergence of these bacteria produces gas, which can cause bloating and diarrhea.

Artificial Sweeteners

With a few notable exceptions, artificial sweeteners can be very dangerous to children.

Stevia. Stevia is the only artificial sweetener that Dr. Cabin recommends for children. Made from a shrub found in South America, it is much sweeter than sugar and has no calories. It hasn't been approved by the FDA because, says an FDA consumer safety officer, " . . . no one has ever provided the FDA with adequate evidence that it is safe." Stevia can be sold as a dietary supplement but not as a sweetener.

The FDA has approved four no-calorie sugar substitutes.

Saccharin. In studies, this substance was linked to cancer in animals and is not recommended by Dr. Cabin.

Aspartame. Aspartame is even more controversial than saccharin. The FDA originally banned it because of a possible link to brain tumors. The ban has since been lifted, however, and the FDA claims that more than 100 studies testify to its safety.

Dr. Cabin says that from his research and observations, he has concluded that aspartame should not be recommended, especially for children. He has observed improvement of pa-

(continued)

tients after taking them off all use of aspartame. Symptoms that improved dramatically included, in order of severity, headaches, memory problems, insomnia, dizziness, and vision problems (including pain and pressure in the eyes). These findings are consistent with symptoms found to be caused by aspartame (along with diarrhea, nightmares, and nausea) in a study. Dr. Cabin advises aspartame users to tell their doctors of this consumption, even if they have no adverse symptoms.

Dr. Cabin worries about aspartame usage because of its chemical properties. Aspartame is made from phenylalanine and aspartic acid. Its ingestion results in the production of methanol, formaldehyde, and formate in the body—substances that could be toxic at high doses. Heating aspartame breaks it down chemically into these possibly harmful chemicals, so it cannot be used for cooking.

Dr. Cabin believes that if this breakdown occurs before we ingest the aspartame, then we are ingesting these chemicals in a more dangerous toxic form. For this reason, aspartame-sweetened diet sodas and other foods that are left outside, unrefrigerated, in hot climates during shipping or manufacturing should never be consumed, he states.

Is just a little bit of aspartame okay for your kids? Research suggests that the answer is no. A recent study has shown that the formaldehyde from aspartame accumulates in high concentrations in the liver and in lower, but still substantial, concentrations in the kidney, brain, and eyes. Dr. Cabin cautions that formaldehyde is very difficult to eliminate from the body and that just small amounts of aspartame consumed over a long period of time could be enough to cause nerve poison.

To learn more about problems associated with aspartame, contact the Consumer Safety Network, PO Box 780634, Dallas, TX 75378-0634.

Acesulfame potassium. I could find no reports of this product causing harmful effects in people who used it. It was judged safe by the FDA in 1988 as a tabletop sweetener, and it's chemically stable enough to be used in cooking.

Sucralose. As of this writing, sucralose sounds very promising. Judged safe by the FDA in "more than 110 animal and human safety studies conducted over 20 years," sucralose is now labeled as an all-purpose sweetener for all foods by the FDA. It cannot be digested and, after being tasted, just passes on out without adding calories to the body or sugar to the blood. It can be used in baking and cooking.

Read Those Labels!

When it comes to sweeteners, reading the fine print can be very important. Be aware of the following cautions.

- Some sweeteners are used in mixtures. Many supposedly sugar-free products add sugars for thickening. For instance, a bottle of granulated stevia I purchased at a health food store contained maltidextrin, a mix of maltitol and dextrin, as a thickening, bulking agent. Eaten in enough quantity, the maltitol part of this product can produce diarrhea. The dextrin can add the same disadvantages as sugar.
- Glycerine, a sweetener synthesized from starch, is often found in supposedly sugar-free foods and can add calories and carbohydrates. You'll often find glycerine in candy, puddings, cookie and cake mixes, and nutrition bars.
- Brown sugar and molasses may be promoted as being more healthful and/or more natural and nutritious than white sugar, but they are still basically sugars in different stages of refinement and should be regarded as such.

The Rude Food Rules

Don't despair if you're feeling a bit overwhelmed by all of the information in this book. It's ideal, of course, to follow the plan to the letter. But we all know that life doesn't always happen on schedule. Fortunately, the most powerful changes you can make in your family's eating habits are also the easiest—and quickest—to achieve.

Here are the fundamental rules that will empower you to improve your family's eating habits and end your children's food-related rudeness.

Rule #1: Serve whole foods. Unadulterated by additives and preservatives, whole foods are foods as nature intended them to be eaten. Make sure your child's diet is rich in whole foods such as fresh fruit and vegetables, whole grains, nuts, seeds, beans and legumes, and fresh meat, eggs, and dairy products.

Rule #2: Eat every 2 to 2½ hours. Eating every few hours will keep your child's blood sugar level stable and help to prevent mood swings.

Rule #3: Limit portion size. Eating huge portions of food overtaxes the body's resources. Limit a serving of meat or fish to 3 to 4 ounces (about the size of a deck of playing cards), and make a portion of vegetables 4 ounces.

Rule #4: Get protein throughout the day. All meals and most

Sickening sweetener. Aspartame is supposed to be a good sugar-substitute for kids. But, according to Dr. Cabin, it has been shown to cause symptoms of nervous system disorders in adults (headaches, depression, hyperactivity, uncontrollable thoughts) and should not be given to children.

Stevia is the better sugar substitute. It's available in many snacks should contain a small portion of the daily protein requirement. Try nuts and dried soy nuts for a protein-rich snack. Do, however, limit the amount of protein your child consumes at dinnertime to no more than one-third of the day's total protein.

Rule #5: Drink at least 64 ounces of water every day. Encourage your child to drink eight 8-ounce glasses of water a day, and more if she's involved in sports. Mineral water from natural springs is best, but filtered water from the tap is fine.

Rule #6: Discourage all uses of refined sugar. Check the labels of all foods your child eats. And be sure to avoid sugar that goes by other names, such as high-fructose corn syrup, maltodextrin, and dextrose.

Rule #7: Accentuate the positive in foods. You don't have to think of yourself as the food police. Instead, focus on the beauty and benefits of healthful foods. Stress the importance of this food in keeping an attractive appearance and in feeling great.

Rule #8: Identify the rudeness as rudeness. It's easy to see rudeness in somebody else's kid, yet overlook it in your own. Make a note of when your child is being rude, and try to identify the types of food that might be triggering the unacceptable behavior.

brands, in both granulated and liquid forms, at health food and natural foods stores. It's not found in sodas or any other kind of commercially sold food.

Diet candy bars. Products sold as diet candy bars may be sweetened with substances such as malitol, which can have a laxative effect. The result can be very violent diarrhea that can be exhausting ssing for your child. Other ingredients to look for and e mannitol and sorbitol.

meat. Lunchmeat is loaded with additives that can make kids feel bad and behave even worse, such as nitrites, food dyes, and sulfites. Nitrites are used to cure meats, especially pork, and are often converted to nitrosamines—very powerful carcinogens—in the body after they're eaten. Sulfites, which are preservatives used to lengthen the shelf life of the product, have now been outlawed for use on fresh foods by the FDA because of their potential to cause severe allergic reactions, especially in the lungs. If you must serve packaged meats, buy turkey and chicken and ham slices in your local health food store or natural foods supermarket. Make sure there are no nitrites, food dyes, or sulfites among the ingredients listed on the label. If you don't have a natural foods market in your area, consult the Resources on page 203 for mail-order sources of natural foods.

beyond nutrition: the AAA method for reversing bad attitude

While food can be the primary culprit in causing your child's bad attitude, often there are also other factors that contribute to your child's rude behaviors.

Some of the most important causes of childhood rudeness include the following factors.

Their peers. Your child's friends might have parents who see rude behavior as cute, think rudeness is admirable (even a sign of independence!), or think it's their fault their kids treat them rudely.

These parents allow, I dare say, *encourage* their children to be rude. Their children's behaviors are examples to your kids.

Their music. Rebellious music has been suspected as a source of bad attitudes since Elvis Presley first shook his hips, and probably before. Say what you want about its cultural significance, its rhythms and vivid images, you still have to admit that much of rock and particularly rap music is rude and glorifies bad attitudes. Today's lyrics and video imagery are more violent and defiant than ever. These powerful messages get through to your children and can lead them to emulate those attitudes.

Their schools. In my research and visits to schools, I have heard one concern raised over and over again from teachers of kindergarten through the 12th grade: Teachers—mainly those in public schools—have no real means of enforcing politeness in students. Principals and other administrators won't back up teachers' attempts to enforce courteous behavior because outraged parents, and sometimes psychologists, will threaten to sue if the teacher dares to try to teach their children to be respectful.

Their bosses. Because of the tremendous need for low-wage workers and the ease with which a teenager can find another job, employers are no longer as quick to enforce codes of conduct in the workplace. I have heard from many employers of teenagers who say that all kinds of behavior must now be endured from these young workers that would not have been put up with 10 years ago.

You, babysitters, your parents, and other relatives. You may be allowing your children to act rudely in your home and not even realizing it. "Sassing" and "talking back" used to be unthinkable in most households up until the 1960s. That's when many child-rearing experts began suggesting that children were "perfect beings." If they were rude and difficult, they were crying out for help in a reaction against bad parenting. The child's rudeness was thus an indictment of the parent. Not wanting to think of themselves as bad parents, many parents found it easier to decide that their kids weren't being rude. As a result, a lot of rudeness in a lot of homes was and still is ignored, overlooked, unacknowledged—

Don't Dismiss These Comments

Children are capable of making all kinds of comments that make you uncomfortable or embarrass you. But sometimes a comment that seems rude at first may really be your child's plea for help. So before you dismiss an uncomfortable comment as rude, consider that it might actually be an expression of a legitimate concern your child has about his life and your relationship.

Here are the kinds of things a child might say that sound rude at first, but are really not:

"Mom, you never spend any time with me."

"Dad, you yell at me (or Mom or someone else) too much."

"Mom, your new boyfriend is not nice."

"Uncle Sid, you get mean to everybody when you have more than two beers."

Why do such comments seem rude at first? Because they're hard to take. But, especially when they're delivered in a respectful tone, you must pay attention to them. The child who makes such comments is usually a very worried child who needs to protect vulnerable loved ones and needs reassurance that things are really all right. They're a sign that your child needs immediate and loving attention.

and so allowed to go on. Perhaps your home is suffering from this denial?

Difficult social and economic conditions. Divorce, the rise of the single-parent family, and the need for both parents to work has caused problems like rudeness in children to go unhandled. Too few parents have had the time, let alone the energy, to teach manners and considerate treatment of others to their kids.

The Rudeness Stops Here

None of the reasons listed above is an excuse to allow your child's rude behavior to go on. All rudeness not caused by food or physiological conditions can be controlled by your child. But he must be taught that such control is necessary. And *you* are the only one who can do it. Now, with a combination of the food and behavioral remedies in this book, you can stop rude behavior once and for all.

Here is an efficient system for handling rudeness in kids: I call it the AAA method. It consists of three parts that should be done swiftly, in sequence, when rudeness occurs—Acknowledge, Announce, and Act.

Here's how to put the AAA method to work in your home.

1. *Acknowledge* the rudeness to yourself and to your child. "That statement, and the tone you used, were rude."
2. *Announce* what you will do or not do because of the rude behavior. "I feel hurt by that remark, so I'm not taking you to the movies today."
3. *Act* on your announcement. Be otherwise engaged in some activity, such as gardening or cooking, when it comes time to take your child to the movies. Disregard any anger this arouses in her. You don't have to justify what you're doing or explain why you're doing it. This action will speak much louder to your child than any words you can say.

If you feel compelled to explain your actions to your child, do so after you've announced your intention to withhold some kind of favor from him. Do not explain anything else but why a comment is rude—as in, "What you said about Uncle Joe being fat hurt his feelings." Be aware, though, that this explanation can engender argument from your child ("I didn't mean to hurt his feelings—

you're crazy!"), and that's what you want to avoid. Your action will be enough to tell her the rudeness is not okay. Don't make this a prolonged debate. It's your perception of the rudeness that matters, and the less you say here the better.

The AAA method works best if you do some preparation first. Sit down with a notebook, and write down all the favors you do for your child or children that show your adoration of them but are not necessary for their immediate survival. The list could include driving them to friends' homes, buying them what they see on commercials, hosting sleepovers for their friends, driving miles and miles every day to a special school for ballet, or paying a tennis coach. Decide which of these services you could choose not to provide on a one-time basis as a result of the child's rude behavior. Remember: The more impact the favor has on the child's social well-being, the more impact it will have as a rudeness curb.

Let's take not driving your child to cheerleading practice. Making the cheerleading squad is a sign of social success in most communities. Missing practice is not done. That's why it could be so effective. Let's see how not driving your child to cheerleading practice works:

The child calls you a dork for not buying her favorite shampoo. "How could you get another brand? You know Curly-Poo is the only kind I use!"

You acknowledge the rudeness. "That statement and that tone are rude, Carla. Rolling your eyes is also rude."

Next, you announce the action you're going to take. You tell her what you're going to do and you do it. "I am not taking you to cheerleading practice today. I'm planting my phlox in the garden instead."

If you'd like, you can explain how Carla's rudeness hurt your feelings. But I advise you not to because the less you say with the

AAA method, the more effective you'll be. Further, explanations often lead to self-pity. "Your rudeness hurts my feelings, Carla. And God knows, I try hard enough to please everybody around here without having to get my feelings hurt because I forgot your Curly-Poo. And anyway, that shampoo costs three times more than our generic brand, and we don't have the kind of money you think we do . . ." and on and on. You're backpedaling trying to defend your actions. The effect of your AAA plan is lost, and Carla has won.

In the "Act" part of this process, there is only one rule: Do what you say you will do. When it's time to go to cheerleading practice, plant your phlox instead. Never mind that Carla's all dressed in her uniform and ready to go. She'll soon figure things out. She insulted you today, so she doesn't go to cheerleading practice today. But if she doesn't treat you rudely tomorrow, she'll get to go as usual. After a few missed practices, she will know you mean business and will control her rude treatment of you—not just on practice day but on other days as well.

Yes, this process will be awful for you. Just keep reminding yourself that it's for your child's own good. Kids need to learn how to treat other people if they're going to be happy in their future lives. With the AAA method, that message is delivered loud and clear, and you shouldn't have to repeat this technique very often.

Identifying Rudeness

The biggest problem most parents seem to have with rudeness is actually identifying it in their own children. It may be quite easy to see in your sister's kids or in the other members of your child's class, but rudeness in your own child can often be explained away with various excuses. Or, after a while, his rudeness may merely be regarded as acceptable communication and not given another thought. That's why most rudeness never gets reversed. Unless you call it by its true name and address it point-blank, this rudeness will linger and sour your child's attitude and personal relationships for years to come.

Below is a list of a variety of rude actions and behaviors that are deliberate and insulting to you and your family. You will probably recognize many of these and already know that they're often combined in a bout of rudeness for maximum effect. When you notice these forms of rudeness, it is your duty to educate your child about the proper way to treat others by employing the AAA method.

Apathetic Rudeness

The child who displays this type of rudeness is your classic passive resister. She has discovered that by saying "I don't care," she can get out of doing anything she doesn't want to do. "I don't care" is her standard response when asked anything:

"How was algebra today, Shirley?"

"I don't know, and I don't really care."

"Shirley, you need to clean your room this weekend. It's really messy."

"I know, I don't care."

Each one of Shirley's responses is rude. They are intended to make the parent feel like a dud who has failed to give meaning to the child's life.

Begging Rudeness

Usually delivered in a whiny voice full of self-pity and guilt-causing despair, this kind of rudeness is recognizable by its litany of "must haves." This child has discovered that by making you think she "needs" everything she wants, she'll usually persuade you to get her what she wants. She may play off your feelings of guilt for supposedly not spending enough time with her or not being able to afford the things her friends get from their parents.

"But I need a new Barbie doll, you promised!" this child may whine. (Even though she already has several baskets full of Barbies and an entire wardrobe of Barbie-sized clothes.)

This kind of rudeness makes a parent feel like a failure because he is unable and/or unwilling to give the child what she says she needs. Children know they cannot get what they want all the time, so their begging rudeness is nothing more than disrespect.

Clinging Rudeness

This child has discovered that by accusing you of abandoning him, he can get you to feel bad, which is always fun. Plus, clinging rudeness often leads to perks like promises of presents and things he wants.

"Mommy, you can't leave me here, I hate it here, don't go."

"But Donald, darling, you're always so happy here when I pick you up."

"No, please, don't leave me here. Take me with you."

"Donnie, sweetheart, I can't do that. I know what! We'll stop on the way home tonight and get you that new Captain Destructo car you've been wanting."

"With the automatic moon-rock digger attachment?"

"All right, with the automatic moon-rock digger. Okay?"

"Okay. I guess."

"Good. Now dry those tears and I'll see you later on."

Clearly, little Donald's behavior is meant to manipulate his mom. What seems like anger and panic is actually rudeness meant to get him what he wants.

Disrespectful Display Rudeness

When your kids purposefully act up with you in front of their friends or make it clear in no uncertain terms that you completely embarrassed them, they are showing their friends that they can disrespect you and get away with it.

"Oh, don't worry," your teenage son says when a friend knocks a bowl of popcorn on the floor. "Mom will clean it up—she loves picking up after me and my friends."

Or, "Mom, please don't wear that dress to school. It's so ugly and out of date. People don't wear stuff like that any more."

Few things are more infuriating than being insulted in front of your child's peers. And once he thinks he can get away with this, you're really beginning to lose your authority. Reclaim it.

Eye-Rolling Rudeness

A lot of eye-rolling and head-shaking is used with this kind of rudeness, also known as Valley Girl Rudeness. Accompanying verbal expressions usually include "duh," "whatever," and "I can't believe you said that!" The intent of this kind of rudeness is to undermine any authority you might have over the child, especially the authority to have her do something she doesn't want to do:

"Megan! I know you know you can't wear that dress to school, it's too short. Go upstairs and change right now."

Megan rolls her eyes and shakes her head. "I can't believe you said that! The other kids laugh at how long this dress is! Duh!"

"Fine, wear it. But if other people talk about you, don't blame me!"

More eye-rolling from Megan at this point, followed by, "Whatever!" as she storms back up to her room to get ready for school.

This form of rudeness is subtle, and many kids get away with it without any repercussions. But it fosters disrespect for you and can lead to more open hostility toward your authority.

Hateful Rudeness

This child tells you he hates you every time you do anything that displeases him. His words are delivered with a fury that often escalates into a raging tantrum. These displays are frightening and unexpected and tend to ruin your mood as well as the mood of anyone within earshot of this rudeness attack. The intent is usually quite simple: The child knows you don't want him to hate you and will give in to just about anything to prevent that possibility.

"Chucky, you know you can't eat popcorn on the new sofa. Please finish it in the kitchen."

"I hate you! You never want me to do anything I want!"

"Of course I don't hate you, Chucky, it's just that I'm worried about the new furniture . . . "

"I won't spill anything, I promise."

"Well, all right. Just be careful. Okay?"

Whenever a child gets you to give in on the reasonable rules you've established for your household, it opens up the floodgates to more bargaining and begging and ongoing battles for control of the house. Don't fall for it.

Intellectually Superior Rudeness

This child is so adept at telling you what's wrong with you and your parenting or housekeeping or investments that he can seem like a consultant you hired to improve your life. His intent is to undermine any belief you might have that you might know more than he does—and can thus tell him what to do.

"Milton, you have to stop waking up late and missing your algebra class. You'll lose your 'A'!"

"Come on, Dad, you just don't know how math works at the middle school level. The good math teachers are all teaching somewhere else, so the teachers we have are faking it. The teacher in this class reads

Corvette magazines while we're supposed to be doing math problems at our desks, and he doesn't care who shows up. You would know that if you really cared about my education—but obviously you don't."

"All right, all right!" Dad throws up his hands in defeat. "Just try not to oversleep and miss any more classes, okay? It really makes your mom very upset."

I had a recent experience with this kind of rudeness when I had to call the university about an insurance problem. The student worker I spoke to (who sounded as though he were about 18) kept demanding to know exactly what I wanted but was not able, or willing, to clarify what he didn't understand. "Lady, just what is your problem?" he kept saying in an ever more rude voice. Finally, I told him my problem was that I was speaking to a student employee who was being rude, and as a result, I wanted to speak to his manager immediately. He became so polite after that, and so helpful, that he seemed like a completely changed person.

This student worker's behavior was typical of the person who tries to show intellectually superior rudeness. He and the child in the above example, Milton, try making the adult seem like a total dud, someone who doesn't know what he's talking about. In order to cope, stay focused on what you're trying to communicate and keep your attention on the behavior you want changed—not on what the child wants to do to dissuade you.

Lewd Rudeness

This kind of rudeness is a bit difficult for me to talk about, and I'm sure you feel uncomfortable reading about it. But it's all too real among kids today. Thanks to a host of factors, such as the abundance of arousing sexual images on television, in movies, and in music lyrics; the increasingly early onset of puberty; and friends who might be sexually active at shockingly young ages, some kids make inappropriately lewd and lascivious comments at the most inappropriate times, such as at family dinners, when company is visiting, and especially when they are with their friends.

Lewd rudeness can be manifested in language (such as the use of the "F" word in every other sentence) and imagery and comments on your appearance and those of others in your family or neighborhood. Teachers I interviewed said they had observed this kind of shocking rudeness in children as young as 6 years old.

Some kids actually don't know that lewdness is rude. They might have to be told several times before they fully comprehend the category of speech that is lewd and thus rude:

"Look at the ____ on that ____!"

"Rick, that kind of talk is inappropriate."

"Oh, Mom, Mrs. Endicott looks so hot in those new red shorts. Mmmm, she's fine."

"Rick, that kind of observation is unacceptable and inappropriate, and I don't want you using that kind of language again."

The intent of this kind of rudeness is usually to shock, to express inappropriate desires, or to mimic others' actions. If Rick asks why his observation is unacceptable and inappropriate, tell him that it is demeaning and sexual in nature, and comments like that are unacceptable in your family.

Mean Rudeness

This child appears to have no compassion for anyone and doesn't care about any person's feelings or well-being other than his own. The intent of mean rudeness is enjoying the power the child feels at making others embarrassed and upset:

"Grandma Sue, Mom said you're getting fat."

"Billy, I never said that," Mom says.

"Yes you did, Mom, you said it at dinner just last Tuesday."

Or consider this example:

"Dad, Mark's father earns three times as much as you do. What happened to you?"

"Mark's dad has more education than I do," Dad explains.

"I guess he's just smarter than you, huh?"

This type of rudeness is meant to provoke you and put you on the defensive in order to shift power into your child's hands. The less respect he shows for you, he believes, the less he needs to follow your rules.

Offensive Rudeness

This child offends every chance he gets. He offends with insults and with gross remarks. Such comments are never even remotely funny, just reminiscent of Howard Stern in their power to offend. There's no point in telling this child he's being offensively rude— he already knows that and is savoring it to the hilt.

"That dog of yours looks like a big, bloated, blood-sucking tick!"

"Your stomach hangs over your bathing suit, Uncle Ned. Oooh, gross!"

The child must be taught that jokes are not made at the expense of others and that empathy for others is something that is valued in your family.

Polite Rudeness

Coming from a wealthy dowager at a fussy-lady tea party, this kind of rudeness has to be endured. But from a child trying to put on airs, it does not.

"You wouldn't like it in Vail," my cousin's child recently told a less well-off friend of the family, "because you don't know how to ski. And from the looks of your clothes, I'd say you really couldn't afford the kind of ski gear they wear up there."

Another example? "Your hair looks nice combed that way, Uncle Sid," I heard a 9-year-old saying sweetly at a family party. "But I can still see your bald spot. You should try scalp implants like my dad just had."

Again, it's important to stress that in your family, you try not to hurt others' feelings or speak in a way that might make them feel bad. It's a lesson your children won't get from anyone else, so it's important they learn it from you.

Sullen Rudeness

Also called lazy rudeness, this is one of the most annoying kinds of all. It usually rears its head in the preteen years and, unless dealt with, will continue for as long as the child shares your home. It is very much like apathetic rudeness except that it's a bit more combative in tone.

"You can't make me," the child says when asked to do anything at all, such as getting off the couch for 10 minutes and taking a walk around the block. Other responses might include "Do it yourself" or "Why do I always have to be the one to do that?" Or just "Oooh. I don't think so," in a tone of voice so obnoxious you have to grit your teeth. He then returns to his video game or television show in a way that indicates you've been dismissed.

Your child wants to just tune you out, to make you irrelevant. Stay connected to him and you'll both be better off.

X-treme Rudeness

Also known as sports rudeness or skateboard rudeness, this kind is practiced by kids who believe their sports expertise (or some other kind of skill) takes precedence over anything you or anyone else in the family might care about:

"Mom, I have to be at the park by 10. I *told* you five times I'm in the first event!"

"Dad, I have to use my board in the driveway, where else is there? The road, for God's sake? Jeez."

Don't let your child's activities and interests seem more important than your family life. Help him keep things in perspective.

Discipline with Confidence

Now that you know what rudeness is, you can acknowledge it without having to think about it. You don't have to worry about whether or not your child's insult is correct or the comment true or the accusation accurate—you know that he is being rude and you do not, and should not, have to put up with it. You can acknowledge the rudeness as unacceptable, announce what you're going to do or not do as a result of it, and follow through (act) on your announcement.

Finally, stop feeling guilty. You are not responsible for your child's decision to be rude. You are only responsible for stopping him from being rude.

part 3

Making It Work
in Your Home

your game plan: a week's worth of menus and recipes

By now, you've learned a lot about the basics of nutrition and how your child's diet affects her behavior. But I suspect you're asking the most common question I get when I talk about these problems:

"So, what should I feed my kid?"

Here are some answers. Together with cooking and nutrition experts at *Prevention* Healthy Cooking books, we pulled together some kitchen-tested recipes that your family will love. Below you'll find a week's menu plan that incorporates these recipes and helps you to meet the nutritional needs of your kids without overloading them with refined sugars and carbohydrates or processed foods. We designed the plan to promote well-being, a positive attitude, and polite, sunny behavior all day long. If you're wondering if your kids will like this food, I think you'll be pleasantly surprised. Give them some credit. With your help and guidance, they can learn to appreciate the richness of these flavors and thrive on their new way of eating. If there's resistance at first, don't give up—your children's health (and your sanity!) depends on it. Keep experimenting with new recipes to find the ones that your kids like best.

Don't lose heart! You *can* get your kids to eat what they should eat and avoid those foods that don't allow them to feel their best. There are more ideas on smart strategies to make these changes stick in chapters 10 and 11.

Meals for Active Children

Refer to "How Much Food Should My Child Eat?" on page 74 to find out how many calories your child should be getting each day. Once you've found that number, choose the meal plan that most closely matches your child's calorie goal, making minor adjustments as necessary.

Day 1

	1,800 calories	2,200 calories	3,000 calories
Breakfast			
Multigrain Cereal (see page 136)	¾ cup	1 cup	2 cups
Soy milk	¾ cup	1 cup	1½ cups
Sliced peaches	½ cup	½ cup	1 cup
Fruited yogurt	8 oz	8 oz	8 oz
Lunch			
Peanut butter and jelly sandwich on whole wheat bread	1	1	1½
Banana	1	1	1
Assorted raw vegetables	½ cup	1 cup	1 cup
Nonfat ranch dressing	2 Tbsp	3 Tbsp	3 Tbsp

	1,800 calories	2,200 calories	3,000 calories
Dinner			
Chicken Drumsticks Roasted with Herbs (see page 137)	½ serving	1 serving	1½ servings
Macaroni and cheese	¾ cup	1¼ cups	1½ cups
Steamed peas and carrots with butter	½ cup	1 cup	1¼ cups
Apple Crumble with Toasted-Oat Topping (see page 138)	1 serving	1 serving	1 serving
Snack			
Frozen nonfat yogurt bar	1	1	1
Daily Total			
Calories	1,842	2,252	3,034
Protein	84	119	162

Day 2

Breakfast			
Breakfast Berry Sundae (see page 139)	1 serving	1 serving	1 serving
Toasted whole wheat English muffin	1	1	2
Jam	2 Tbsp	2 Tbsp	¼ cup
Lunch			
Vegetarian bean soup	1 cup	1 bowl	1 bowl
Turkey breast	3 oz	4 oz	5 oz
Swiss cheese	1 oz	1 oz	1½ oz
Rye bread	2 slices	2 slices	2 slices
Lettuce	1 leaf	1 leaf	1 leaf
Tomato	2 slices	2 slices	2 slices

(continued)

Day 2 *(cont.)*

	1,800 calories	2,200 calories	3,000 calories
Dinner			
Salmon and Couscous Salad with Vegetables (see page 140)	½–1 serving	1 serving	1½ servings
Baked butternut squash	½ cup	1 cup	1 cup
Mixed greens with balsamic vinegar	1 cup	2 cups	3 cups
Sunflower seeds	none	1 oz	2 oz
Whole grain roll	1	1	1
Butter	1 tsp	1 tsp	1 tsp
Snack			
Chocolate-Raspberry Dip and Fresh Fruit (see page 141)	1 serving	1 serving	1 serving
Daily Total			
Calories	1,829	2,279	3,030
Protein	97	126	162

Day 3

	1,800 calories	2,200 calories	3,000 calories
Breakfast			
Peanut Butter and Banana Shake (see page 142)	1	1	1
Granola bar	1	1	2
Granny Smith apple	1	1	1
Lunch			
Vegetarian chili	½ cup	1 cup	1¼ cups
Corn bread	1 slice	2 slices	2 slices

	1,800 calories	2,200 calories	3,000 calories
Shredded cabbage salad	1 cup	1 cup	1 cup
Nonfat yogurt dressing	2 Tbsp	2 Tbsp	2 Tbsp
Vegetable juice	¾ cup	¾ cup	1¼ cups

Dinner

	1,800 calories	2,200 calories	3,000 calories
Pork and Pepper Stir-Fry (see page 142)	1 serving	1 serving	1½ servings
Brown basmati rice	⅓ cup	⅔ cup	1 cup
Steamed greens and carrots	1 cup + 1 tsp flax oil	2 cups + 1 tsp flax oil	3 cups + 2 tsp flax oil
Broiled Pineapple with Ginger-Yogurt Sauce (see page 143)	1 serving	1 serving	1 serving + 2 oz walnuts

Snack

	1,800 calories	2,200 calories	3,000 calories
Rice cake or popcorn	1 rice cake	2 cups popcorn + 1 tsp flax oil	3 cups popcorn + 2 tsp flax oil

Daily Total

	1,800 calories	2,200 calories	3,000 calories
Calories	1,799	2,235	3,066
Protein	85	100	120

Day 4

Breakfast

	1,800 calories	2,200 calories	3,000 calories
Egg white omelette with vegetables	2 egg whites + ¼ cup veggies	3 egg whites + ¼ cup veggies	4 egg whites + ½ cup veggies
Oat toast	1 slice	2 slices	2 slices
Orange marmalade	1 Tbsp	2 Tbsp	2 Tbsp

(continued)

Day 4 (cont.)

	1,800 calories	2,200 calories	3,000 calories
Lunch			
Texas Burrito (see page 144)	½ serving	1 serving	1 serving
Spicy Oven Fries (see page 145)	1 serving	1 serving	2 servings
Baby spinach salad	1 cup	2 cups	2 cups
Creamy herb dressing	1 Tbsp	2 Tbsp	3 Tbsp
Dinner			
Whole Grain Caprese Pasta (see page 146)	1 serving	1¼ servings	1½ servings
Tuna Salad in Lettuce Wrappers (see page 147)	2 wrappers	3 wrappers	4 wrappers
Snack			
Sliced strawberries with kiwifruit	½–1 cup	1 cup	2 cups
Nonfat chocolate pudding	½ cup	¾ cup	1¼ cups
Daily Total			
Calories	1,819	2,190	2,991
Protein	87	137	170

Day 5

	1,800 calories	2,200 calories	3,000 calories
Breakfast			
Rich 'n' Creamy Brown Rice Pudding (see page 147)	1 serving	1 serving	2 servings
Sliced fruit	¾ cup	1¼ cups	1½ cups

	1,800 calories	**2,200 calories**	**3,000 calories**
Lunch			
Vegetarian split pea soup	1 cup	1 bowl	1 bowl
Grilled Tomato and Cheese Sandwiches (see page 148)	1 serving	1½ servings	2 servings
Mixed greens salad	1 cup	2 cups	3 cups
Croutons and vinaigrette	1 Tbsp each	2 Tbsp each	3 Tbsp each
Dinner			
Baked Salmon with Oregano (see page 149)	1 serving	1 serving	1 serving
Rotini with marinara sauce	1 cup	1½ cups	2¼ cups
Steamed baby asparagus	4 spears	6 spears	8 spears
Creamy dill dressing	1 Tbsp	1 Tbsp	2 Tbsp
Whole grain roll	1	1	1
Butter	1 tsp	1 tsp	1 tsp
Snack			
Berry-Good Smoothie (see page 149)	1 serving	1 serving	2 servings
Award-Winning Banana Bread (see page 150)	1 slice	1½ slices	2 slices
Daily Total			
Calories	1,822	2,179	3,025
Protein	81	108	124

Multigrain Cereal

2   cups rolled oats

2   cups wheat flakes

2   cups malted barley flakes

2   cups rye flakes

1   box (1 pound) dark or golden raisins

1½   cups flaxseeds, ground

¾   cup sesame seeds

In an airtight container, combine the oats, wheat flakes, barley flakes, rye flakes, raisins, flaxseeds, and sesame seeds. Store in the freezer until ready to use.

To cook: For 1 serving, bring 1 cup water to a boil in a small saucepan. Add a pinch of salt. Add ⅓ cup of the cereal, cover, and cook, stirring occasionally, for 25 minutes, or until thickened and creamy.

For 4 servings, use 3 cups water, ¼ teaspoon salt, and 1½ cups cereal. Cook for 25 to 30 minutes.

Makes thirty-six ⅓-cup servings

Per serving: 16 calories, 5 g protein, 29 g carbohydrates, 4 g fat, 0 mg cholesterol, 5 g dietary fiber, 8 mg sodium

Chicken Drumsticks Roasted with Herbs

2   tablespoons whole wheat flour

1   teaspoon dried oregano

1   teaspoon dried thyme

¾   teaspoon dried dillweed or dill seed

½   teaspoon dried savory or rosemary, crumbled

½   teaspoon paprika

1   teaspoon onion powder

1   teaspoon salt

½   teaspoon ground black pepper

8   skinless chicken drumsticks (about 5 ounces each)

1   tablespoon olive oil

Preheat the oven to 425°F. Generously coat a baking sheet with cooking spray.

In a bowl, mix together the flour, oregano, thyme, dill, savory or rosemary, paprika, onion powder, salt, and pepper. Coat the chicken with the oil. Sprinkle with the herbed flour, toss to coat, and press the flour onto the drumsticks.

Preheat the prepared baking sheet for 5 minutes. Arrange the drumsticks on the sheet, leaving at least 1" between each. Roast, turning occasionally, until the chicken is browned and crisp, the juices run clear, and a meat thermometer registers 180°F, 30 to 35 minutes.

Makes 4 servings

Per serving: 228 calories, 30 g protein, 4 g carbohydrates, 10 g fat, 97 mg cholesterol, 1 g dietary fiber, 682 mg sodium

Note: Instead of using all whole wheat flour, you can combine 1 tablespoon soy flour and 1 tablespoon whole wheat flour. Use 4 legs left in one piece or separate the thighs from the drumsticks. Serve with 1 cup tomato sauce.

Apple Crumble with Toasted-Oat Topping

6   medium Jonagold or Golden Delicious apples, cored and
     thinly sliced

½   cup unsweetened applesauce

¾   cup rolled oats

3   tablespoons toasted wheat germ

3   tablespoons packed light brown sugar

1   teaspoon ground cinnamon

1   tablespoon canola oil

1   tablespoon unsalted butter, cut into small pieces

Preheat the oven to 350°F. Coat a 13" x 9" baking dish with
cooking spray.

Combine the apples and applesauce in the prepared baking dish.

In a small bowl, combine the oats, wheat germ, brown sugar, and
cinnamon. Add the oil and butter. Mix with your fingers to form crumbs.
Sprinkle the oat mixture evenly over the apples.

Bake for 30 minutes, or until the topping is golden and the apples
are bubbling.

Makes 6 servings

Per serving: 207 calories, 3 g protein, 38 g carbohydrates, 6 g fat, 5 mg cholesterol, 6 g dietary fiber, 3 mg sodium

Note: Although you can make this recipe with peeled apples, leaving the peels on
ensures that you get more fiber as well as the beneficial antioxidant quercetin.

Breakfast Berry Sundaes

2   cups plain yogurt

½   teaspoon vanilla extract

2   teaspoons toasted wheat germ (optional)

½   teaspoon ground cinnamon

3   tablespoons dried cranberries or cherries

3   tablespoons granola or muesli

2   cups blueberries (1 pint)

3   tablespoons toasted pecans, chopped

Divide the yogurt among 4 bowls, reserving ¼ cup. Drizzle the vanilla over the yogurt in each bowl and sprinkle with the wheat germ (if using) and cinnamon. Scatter the cranberries or cherries and granola or muesli over each. Spoon the blueberries over the granola or muesli, and top each serving with 1 tablespoon of the remaining yogurt. Sprinkle with the pecans.

Makes 4 servings

Per serving: 200 calories, 6 g protein, 24 g carbohydrates, 10 g fat, 16 mg cholesterol, 3 g dietary fiber, 63 mg sodium

Salmon and Couscous Salad with Vegetables

1   skinless salmon fillet (1 pound), 1" thick

3   tablespoons + 1 teaspoon olive oil

¾   teaspoon salt

¼   teaspoon ground black pepper

20   spears (10 ounces) fresh or frozen thin asparagus, thawed if frozen and cut into ½" lengths

1   zucchini (6 ounces), halved lengthwise and thinly sliced

1   clove garlic, minced

¾   cup water

⅔   cup whole wheat couscous

2–3 teaspoons red wine vinegar or lemon juice

Preheat the oven to 375°F. Rub the salmon with 1 teaspoon of the olive oil and season with ¼ teaspoon of the salt and ⅛ teaspoon of the pepper. Arrange in a shallow baking dish and bake just until the salmon is cooked through but still juicy, 20 to 25 minutes. Let cool until easy to handle, 5 to 10 minutes. Break into large flakes.

Heat the remaining 3 tablespoons olive oil in a large saucepan over medium heat. Add the asparagus, zucchini, and garlic. Cook, stirring occasionally, until crisp-tender, 3 to 5 minutes. Add the water, the remaining ½ teaspoon salt, and the remaining ⅛ teaspoon pepper. Simmer for 2 to 3 minutes over medium heat. Bring to a boil and stir in the couscous. Cover, remove from the heat, and let sit 5 minutes.

Fluff the couscous with a fork, remove to a large bowl, and season with the vinegar or lemon juice. Cool slightly and fold in the salmon. Serve warm, at room temperature, or chilled.

Makes 4 servings

Per serving: 397 calories, 29 g protein, 28 g carbohydrates, 19 g fat, 62 mg cholesterol, 3 g dietary fiber, 543 mg sodium

Note: If desired, you can replace the fresh salmon with 2 cups of canned salmon. You can also make this salad up to 3 days ahead and store it in a covered container in the refrigerator.

Chocolate-Raspberry Dip and Fresh Fruit

⅓   cup raspberry fruit spread

2   tablespoons unsweetened cocoa powder

2   tablespoons milk

½   cup sour cream

2   teaspoons vanilla extract

2   teaspoons raspberry liqueur (optional)

6   drops liquid stevia

1   tablespoon chopped walnuts

1   large navel orange, peeled and segmented

1   pear, cut lengthwise into ½" slices

1   apple, cut lengthwise into ½" slices

½   pint strawberries, with hulls left on

In a small saucepan, mix the fruit spread, cocoa, and milk. Cook over low heat, stirring occasionally, until the cocoa has dissolved and the fruit spread has melted, 1 to 2 minutes. Remove to a bowl, cover, and let cool to room temperature.

Place the sour cream in a serving bowl and gradually stir in the cocoa mixture, vanilla extract, liqueur (if using), and stevia. Sprinkle with the nuts and place on a platter.

Arrange the orange, pear, apple, and strawberries around the bowl.

Makes 6 servings

Per serving: 147 calories, 2 g protein, 24 g carbohydrates, 5 g fat, 9 mg cholesterol, 3 g dietary fiber, 17 mg sodium

Note: The raspberry flavor in this chocolate dip becomes more pronounced after a day or two. To make the dip ahead, store in a covered container in the refrigerator for up to 5 days. Let the dip come to room temperature before serving. To keep the dip warm, place the bowl in a larger bowl filled with boiling water and replenish the hot water as needed.

Peanut Butter and Banana Shake

1　cup (8 ounces) fat-free plain yogurt

1　frozen banana

1　tablespoon creamy peanut butter

1　teaspoon vanilla extract

1　teaspoon honey

½　teaspoon ground cinnamon

In a blender, combine yogurt, banana, peanut butter, vanilla extract, honey, and cinnamon. Blend until smooth.

Makes 1

Per shake: 366 calories, 18 g protein, 55 g carbohydrates, 9 g fat, 4 mg cholesterol, 3 g dietary fiber, 252 mg sodium

Pork and Pepper Stir-Fry

2　tablespoons apricot all-fruit spread

2　tablespoons soy sauce

½　teaspoon crushed red-pepper flakes

1　pound pork tenderloin, cut into ½" strips

4　teaspoons canola oil

½　cup chicken or vegetable broth

1　tablespoon cornstarch

6　cloves garlic, thinly sliced

1　tablespoon grated fresh ginger

2　large red bell peppers, cut into thin strips

2　large green bell peppers, cut into thin strips

1　large onion, cut into wedges

In a medium bowl, combine the all-fruit spread, 1 tablespoon of the soy sauce, and ¼ teaspoon of the red-pepper flakes. Add the pork and toss to coat well. Cover and marinate for 20 minutes at room temperature.

Heat 2 teaspoons of the oil in a large nonstick skillet over high heat. Add the pork mixture and cook, stirring frequently, for 3 minutes, or until the pork is slightly pink in the center. Place in a bowl and keep warm. Wipe the skillet with a paper towel.

In a cup, whisk together the broth and cornstarch and set aside.

Add the remaining 2 teaspoons oil to the same skillet and place over medium-high heat. Add the garlic, ginger, and the remaining ¼ teaspoon red-pepper flakes and cook, stirring constantly, for 2 minutes, or until the garlic is golden.

Add the bell peppers, onion, and the remaining 1 tablespoon soy sauce and cook, stirring, for 6 minutes, or until tender.

Add the pork and any accumulated juices to the pepper mixture. Stir the cornstarch mixture and add to the skillet. Cook, stirring constantly, for 1 minute, or until thickened.

Makes 4 servings

Per serving: 285 calories, 27 g protein, 25 g carbohydrates, 9 g fat, 74 mg cholesterol, 4 g dietary fiber, 665 mg sodium

Broiled Pineapple with Ginger-Yogurt Sauce

½ cup plain yogurt
1½ teaspoons chopped crystallized ginger
1 teaspoon vanilla extract
1 teaspoon grated orange peel
2 tablespoons butter
1 tablespoon + 1½ teaspoons lime juice
2 tablespoons unsweetened peach or apricot fruit spread
½ cored, peeled pineapple, cut into wedges 1½" thick

Position the oven rack 4" from the heat source and preheat the broiler.

In a small bowl, combine the yogurt, ginger, vanilla extract, and orange peel. Cover and set aside.

(continued)

In a small skillet, combine the butter, lime juice, and fruit spread. Cook over low heat until the butter and fruit spread are melted. Place the pineapple in a broiler-safe 11" x 7" baking pan. Pour the butter mixture over the wedges and toss to coat. Arrange in a single layer.

Broil, turning once, until lightly browned on both sides, 5 to 7 minutes, shaking the pan occasionally so the juice doesn't burn. Remove the wedges and juice to 4 bowls, and serve hot or warm topped with the yogurt sauce.

Makes 4 servings

Per serving: 124 calories, 1 g protein, 15 g carbohydrates, 7 g fat, 19 mg cholesterol, 1 g dietary fiber, 76 mg sodium

Texas Burrito

3	tablespoons vegetable oil
1½	pounds boneless stew beef, cut into ½" cubes
1	onion, chopped
2	cloves garlic, minced
1–1½	small jalapeño chile peppers, seeded and finely chopped (wear plastic gloves when handling)
1	tablespoon + 1½ teaspoons chili powder
2	teaspoons ground cumin
½	teaspoon salt
¼	teaspoon ground black pepper
1	tablespoon tomato paste
1¼	cups hot water or beef broth
8	whole wheat tortillas (6")
1	cup (4 ounces) shredded Monterey Jack cheese
4	large lettuce leaves, shredded (optional)
1	large ripe tomato, finely chopped

Heat the oil in a saucepan over medium-high heat. Working in batches, add the beef and cook, stirring, until browned, 5 to 8 minutes. Remove to a plate. Reduce the heat to medium. Return the beef to the pan and stir in the onion, garlic, and jalapeño peppers. Cook, stirring occasionally, until the vegetables start to soften, about 5 minutes. Stir in the chili powder, cumin, salt, and black pepper.

In a cup, combine the tomato paste and water or broth. Stir into the beef mixture. Reduce the heat to low. Cover and cook, stirring occasionally, for 1 hour. Remove the lid and cook until the beef is tender, 30 minutes.

Meanwhile, preheat the oven to 375°F and wrap the tortillas in foil. Bake until steaming and pliable, 5 to 10 minutes.

To assemble each burrito, place a tortilla on a work surface and arrange a line of cheese down the center. Top with the beef mixture, lettuce (if using), and tomato. Fold two opposite sides over the filling, then fold one of the remaining sides over to enclose.

Makes 4 servings (8 burritos)

Per serving: 603 calories, 50 g protein, 48 g carbohydrates, 28 g fat, 129 mg cholesterol, 6 g dietary fiber, 897 mg sodium

Note: For a quick meal, make a double batch of the filling and refrigerate or freeze it. Store in a covered container in the refrigerator for up to 5 days or in the freezer for up to 2 months. To reheat, thaw in the refrigerator, then cook in a saucepan over low heat, stirring occasionally, until heated through, about 10 minutes.

Spicy Oven Fries

2   medium russet potatoes, scrubbed and cut into long ¼"-thick strips

1   tablespoon canola oil

1   tablespoon roasted garlic and red pepper spice blend

¼   teaspoon salt

¼   teaspoon freshly ground black pepper

Preheat the oven to 425°F. Coat a 13" x 9" baking pan with cooking spray.

Place the potatoes in a mound in the prepared baking pan and

(continued)

sprinkle with the oil, spice blend, salt, and pepper. Toss to coat well. Spread the potatoes in a single layer.

Bake, turning the potatoes several times, for 40 minutes, or until crisp and lightly browned.

Makes 4 servings

Per serving: 115 calories, 3 g protein, 18 g carbohydrates, 4 g fat, 0 mg cholesterol, 2 g dietary fiber, 144 mg sodium

Whole Grain Caprese Pasta

1	pound whole wheat pasta shapes, such as twists
1	cup (8 ounces) fat-free plain yogurt
1	tablespoon + 1 teaspoon extra-virgin olive oil
½	teaspoon salt
1	large clove garlic
1	cup packed fresh basil + additional for garnish
2	large tomatoes, chopped
1	teaspoon balsamic or red wine vinegar
6	ounces reduced-fat mozzarella cheese, cubed

Prepare the pasta according to package directions.

Meanwhile, place the yogurt, oil, salt, and garlic in a blender. Puree until smooth. Add the basil and puree until completely blended.

Place the tomatoes in a small bowl. Toss with the vinegar and add the cheese.

Place the pasta in a large serving bowl. Top with the basil sauce and tomato mixture. Garnish with additional basil.

Makes 5 servings

Per serving: 495 calories, 26 g protein, 72 g carbohydrates, 13 g fat, 20 mg cholesterol, 9 g dietary fiber, 431 mg sodium

Tuna Salad in Lettuce Wrappers

2   cans (6 ounces each) water-packed tuna, drained
¼   cup mayonnaise
1   teaspoon Dijon mustard
1   tablespoon lemon juice
2   tablespoons finely chopped red bell pepper or celery
2   teaspoons capers, drained
2   scallions, thinly sliced
¼   teaspoon salt
⅛   teaspoon ground black pepper
8   large lettuce leaves, such as Boston or leaf

In a bowl, flake the tuna with a fork. Stir in the mayonnaise, mustard, and lemon juice. Stir in the bell pepper or celery, capers, scallions, salt, and pepper. Arrange the lettuce on a work surface with the rib end closest to you and the "cup" facing up. Spoon the tuna salad onto the leaf near the rib end and roll to enclose.

Makes 4 servings

Per 2 wrappers: 222 calories, 21 g protein, 2 g carbohydrates, 14 g fat, 46 mg cholesterol, 1 g dietary fiber, 621 mg sodium

Note: For a change of pace, you can substitute canned or cooked salmon or boneless, skinless sardines for the tuna. Add 1 chopped hard-cooked egg and ½ teaspoon dried dill to the salad. You can also add 3 or 4 thin slices of apple or a slice of Swiss or mozzarella cheese to the wrap.

Rich 'n' Creamy Brown Rice Pudding

3   cups vanilla soy milk
½   cup brown rice
½   teaspoon salt
¼   teaspoon freshly grated nutmeg
2   eggs, lightly beaten
½   cup dried cherries

In a medium saucepan, combine the milk, rice, salt, and nutmeg. Bring to a boil over high heat. Reduce the heat to low, cover, and simmer for 45 minutes. Remove from the heat and let cool for 5 minutes.

Stir ½ cup of the rice mixture into the eggs, stirring constantly. Gradually stir the egg mixture into the saucepan. Stir in the cherries.

Place over medium-low heat and cook, stirring constantly, for 5 minutes, or until thickened. Serve warm or refrigerate to serve cold later.

Makes 4 servings

Per serving: 242 calories, 11 g protein, 38 g carbohydrates, 7 g fat, 106 mg cholesterol, 3 g dietary fiber, 347 mg sodium

Grilled Tomato and Cheese Sandwiches

8   slices multigrain bread

8   slices low-fat Jarlsberg or Cheddar cheese

1   large tomato, cut into 8 slices

2   roasted red peppers, halved

12 large leaves fresh basil

Coat both sides of the bread with olive oil–flavored cooking spray. In a large nonstick skillet over medium heat, cook the bread on 1 side for 2 minutes, or until lightly toasted. Do this in batches, if necessary. Remove from the pan.

Arrange 4 of the slices, toasted side up, on a work surface. Top with the cheese, tomato, peppers, and basil. Top with the remaining bread slices, toasted side down.

Carefully place the sandwiches in the skillet. Cook for 2 minutes per side, or until toasted and the cheese melts.

Makes 4 servings

Per serving: 264 calories, 22 g protein, 33 g carbohydrates, 6 g fat, 20 mg cholesterol, 6 g dietary fiber, 451 mg sodium

Baked Salmon with Oregano

2 teaspoons olive oil

4 skinless salmon fillets (6 ounces each), each 1" thick

1 tablespoon + 1½ teaspoons lemon juice

1 teaspoon dried oregano

½ teaspoon salt

¼ teaspoon ground black pepper

1 tablespoon butter, cut into small pieces

1 teaspoon chopped fresh parsley (optional)

Preheat the oven to 375°F.

Use the oil to grease a shallow baking dish that is large enough to fit the fillets in a single layer. Arrange the fish in the dish and turn to coat with the oil. Sprinkle with the lemon juice, oregano, salt, and pepper. Dot with the butter and cover with foil.

Bake until the fish is cooked through but still very juicy, 20 to 24 minutes. Serve topped with the pan juices and parsley (if using).

Makes 4 servings

Per serving: 290 calories, 34 g protein, 1 g carbohydrates, 16 g fat, 101 mg cholesterol, 0 g dietary fiber, 395 mg sodium

Note: Make this dish ahead or make extras for fast meals. Store extra portions in a covered container in the refrigerator for up to 3 days. To reheat, arrange the fillets in a baking dish, cover, and bake at 350°F until heated through, 5 to 8 minutes. Or serve the fillets cold or at room temperature mixed with vinegar and oil for a fish salad.

Berry-Good Smoothie

1 cup fresh or thawed frozen blueberries

1 cup (8 ounces) vanilla yogurt

½ cup cran-blueberry juice

In a blender, combine the blueberries, yogurt, and cran-blueberry juice. Blend until smooth.

(continued)

Makes 2 servings

Per serving: 184 calories, 5 g protein, 38 g carbohydrates, 2 g fat, 6 mg cholesterol, 2 g dietary fiber, 78 mg sodium

Award-Winning Banana Bread

2	eggs
⅔	cup light butter, melted
1	cup mashed bananas (about 2 large)
⅓	cup milk
1	teaspoon vanilla extract
2½	cups whole wheat flour
1	teaspoon baking soda
½	teaspoon salt
1	teaspoon stevia powder
½	cup chopped nuts

Preheat the oven to 350°F. Combine the eggs, butter, bananas, milk, and vanilla.

In a large bowl, combine the flour, baking soda, salt, stevia powder, and nuts. Add the banana mixture to the dry ingredients. Mix until moistened. Pour into a greased 9" x 5" loaf pan. Bake for 1 hour, or until a wooden pick inserted in the center comes out clean. Remove from pan. Cool and serve.

Makes 20 slices

Per slice: 91 calories, 3 g protein, 14 g carbohydrates, 4 g fat, 11 mg cholesterol, 2 g dietary fiber, 135 mg sodium

9

helping kids deal with problem food situations

Until they become used to eating a healthful diet, encouraging our children to follow the meal plans we have carefully selected for them can be challenging enough. But when special occasions such as holidays and parties come along, eating healthfully becomes an even greater challenge. Plus, we can't shelter our children in the security of our homes forever. They need to learn to interact successfully with other kids and adults. And they have to travel, play in sports, eat out, and be on their own at some point (unless they really want to stay with us right up until we go into the nursing home!).

Probably the single most important thing you can do to get your child to accept this healthy new approach to eating is to change your own mindset. Instead of thinking about how bad it's going to be to give up all sorts of foods, think about how good it will be to enjoy new foods and a newly happy child. This positive thinking is critical to keeping your child from obsessing about what she can't have and to helping her to learn to love the new foods she will be discovering along with you.

Below are some ideas for helping your child deal with special occasions where eating the wrong types of food is especially tempting. By following these practical strategies, you will help him to sail through difficult situations without resorting to eating foods that might cause him harm and start him back on the cycle of food-related bad attitude and rudeness.

The Candy Holidays

The idea of celebrating special occasions with sweets is not a new one. Throughout history, adults gave children sweets on Christmas and other holidays. The difference was that in the past, the amount of sugar, especially white sugar, eaten during the year by children was so low that these sugar treats really were special. In America today, however, we eat so much white sugar (about 156 pounds a year per person—or 3 pounds per week—according to the Department of Agriculture) that children can easily go into sugar-overload mode at special occasions featuring sweet treats. They can feel sick and become rude, mean, and impossible to live with for hours afterward.

Your child does not have to be one of these unhappy, up-and-down, miserable children. He can get through special occasions without overdosing on the sweets *du jour*. How? The answers depend a lot on the situations. Here are some of the most common problem situations and ways of dealing with them.

Birthday Parties

Consider this example of a typical birthday party attended recently by the 8-year-old daughter of a friend in Los Angeles: A grown-up dressed like a fairy queen organized games and gave out chocolate hearts for prizes. Of course, all guests won a prize for something. After the games and the eating of prizes came the cake—a seven-layered fantasy with pink and white whipped cream icing between layers and covering the top, which was also adorned with lacy webs of pink cotton candy. At every place at the table was a small pink wicker basket filled with red and pink foil-wrapped candies. With the cake, striped red and white ice cream was served in large bowls with Pepsi, regular and diet, and strawberry soda. Individual heart-shaped cakes were given out at the end of the party for siblings who had not been invited. The mother of the birthday girl had also planned to serve chocolate mousse with whipped cream but decided it would be a bit much along with the other food.

You do not have to give this kind of birthday party for your child!

When you host a children's or teen's party, concentrate on the activity, not the food. Anything featuring physical activity will be great. Horseback riding, a ballet demonstration and mini class (hire real ballerinas from a local dance studio), a football demonstration and class (hire local high school or college football players to give a little clinic on skills or the rules), and that old standby miniature golf are always great.

For food, serve pizza and salad purchased from the healthiest pizza restaurant in town. (Call around to find one that makes their crust with unrefined flour, cooks with fresh ingredients, and uses high-quality olive oil.) The birthday cake and icing can be made with stevia instead of sugar, and the drinks can be low-sugar or stevia-sweetened real lemonade (no drinks with food dyes, please). (When experimenting with stevia, be sure to start with a small amount first. Just ⅛ teaspoon of liquid stevia is equivalent to ½ cup of sugar. For recipes for treats made with stevia, see pages 141 and 150.)

When your child is a guest at a birthday party, tell the host ahead of time to please limit your child's intake of cake, ice cream, and caffeinated soda; no second portions should be allowed. Your child might even be able to limit his intake himself. If he really has a problem with refined sugar and flour, send foods he can snack on, such as protein bars, along with him. And make sure he doesn't go to the party hungry, so he won't be tempted to dig in to the candy when he arrives.

Halloween

Ah, Halloween. First, you buy bags of candy for the trick-or-treaters, some of which you and your kids eat before Halloween even arrives. Then your children go out to gather more goodies when they trick-or-treat. Any candy left over is consumed by you and your kids the next day. Halloween parties in school and at friends' homes and public places such as parks and recreation centers add even more sugary treats. Only the apples retrieved by bobbing offer any nourishment at all! Your kids—and everyone else's—are likely to have such a lingering addiction to candy that you'll suffer through rudeness for days, even weeks, after Halloween is over.

Here are some ways to take the rudeness-causing foods out of this holiday for your children.

- Concentrate on their costumes. Encourage the making of homemade creations that engage creativity and design talent.
- Give toys or jewelry or movie passes to trick-or-treaters at your home instead of candy. Make the giving out of your treats the

primary focus of the evening, so that the time you spend out with your child collecting treats is limited.

- When you do go collecting treats, use a very small bag or basket to collect. This will make it seem fuller and give your child a sense of accomplishment for filling it up.
- Fill up your child with a healthful dinner before he goes out trick-or-treating—and don't let him eat any candy until he gets home. Then, let him eat a few pieces of his stash—but not enough to set up a sugar craving—and throw out the rest. (Yes, that sounds harsh—but what else can you do?) Explain to your child that your family understands other people eat a lot of candy, but we don't.

Valentine's Day

The last children's Valentine's Day party a mom told me about featured edible hearts of every conceivable confectionary kind—sugar hearts with love sayings, chocolate hearts with cherry centers, marzipan hearts in every color, and pastry hearts with cream-filled centers iced in butter cream and chocolate glaze. Cappuccinos topped with pink whipped cream were served to everyone, even the children (they loved the idea of having such a grown-up drink), and the pièce de résistance was an individual crème brûlée dessert served in a heart-shaped dish to each guest, with second and third helpings of this delicacy not only allowed but urged upon the attendees. This party was, the mom reported, just gorgeous in a visual sense. Yes, the kids did get hyper and difficult early on, but the cappuccino seemed to calm them down.

Clearly, this was a party with the typical sweets-and-caffeine cycle: First, kids were made crazy from too much sugar and then restored (albeit temporarily) in spirits and good behavior with caffeine.

For a more healthful celebration, try this way of celebrating Valentine's Day at your house: Instead of candy, make homemade card creations with your kids for relatives and friends who live alone and tend to be neglected most of the year or who are in nursing homes. Have kids create salads featuring as many red veggies as they can think of—radishes, tomatoes, radicchio—and desserts or smoothies containing reddish fruits, such as strawberries, apples, and raspberries. Whipped cream is fine for toppings in small servings, if sweetened with stevia. Use strawberries, fresh or unsweetened frozen, for making the whipped cream pink, not red food dye.

Easter

A little cousin's third Easter was celebrated with the arrival of one candy-filled Easter basket after another, all from relatives competing to see who could provide the biggest basket—as well as the most enormous chocolate bunny, the most elaborately decorated chocolate cream-filled egg, the fattest marshmallow chick. I had never seen such huge and detailed confectionary delights. The adults and children in the family gorged on these goodies all day and were, I must confess, a lot less happy by evening than they had been when the day started out. My little cousin and her toddler sister are still receiving these baskets filled with sugar-sculpture treats on Easter morning, as are most of the other children in the United States.

What to do? First of all, if you're Christian and so inclined, you may want to spend some time with your kids talking about what this holiday, as well as Christmas, is really about. (You can even explain to them that Jesus, the person for whom Easter and Christmas are celebrated, never got much candy at all in his short life. He had other concerns more important than collecting candy eggs and putting together the biggest and most elaborate basket of all.) Even if you're not Christian or not religious, you and your kids can think of ways to celebrate the coming of springtime that avoid refined sugar. Create baskets filled with healthful treats from the natural foods supermarket or the health food store. If you must have an Easter egg hunt, use plastic eggshells filled with trinkets, meaningful religious gifts, or loose change. I loved glow-in-the-dark crosses, which I attached to the ends of my pigtails, when I was a little girl.

Christmas

Ah, Christmas: A.K.A. the competitive cookie-baking holiday. As early as August, new cookie recipes start appearing in ladies' magazines. By the first week in December, the all-night baking sprees have begun. Cookie batches judged not good enough for giving are designated for immediate family members, especially kids. By Christmas week, trays full of exquisite cookie creations covered with festive wrappings and topped with huge bows are taken to the homes of friends and relatives—to be placed on a sideboard or dining room table along with dozens of other gift-wrapped trays of cookies brought by other relatives and friends.

After gorging steadily on endless amounts of cookies and the Christmas party cakes and pies for about 2 weeks before the Big Day (combined with the anticipation over the unwrapping of the gifts), children are headed for a complete meltdown by Christmas day. Their attitudes can grow so warped that they dislike even their most desired gifts. Wrappings get thrown all over the room, new toys are played with briefly and tossed callously aside, and tantrums are thrown for no reason at all.

Fortunately, there are many ways of celebrating Christmas that won't make kids rude.

- Instead of baking cookies, you could make tree ornaments from papier-mâché or baked clay or jewelry that you pile on a tray and give to the lucky Christmas party hosts (see the Resources on page 205 for a good book on holiday crafts).
- Decorate plain white envelopes that will hold homemade gift certificates for babysitting or yard-raking or other services or gift certificates for movies or other commercial places.
- Stress the philanthropic nature of the holiday to kids by concentrating on making gifts for the less fortunate. Tell your relatives and party guests to bring gifts that are used, or homemade, or funny, or anything else, as long as they do not contain sugar.
- Volunteer to bring a dessert to a potluck or party, then bring fruit cup or a sugarless confection.

School Parties

More sugar is pushed in schools than just about anywhere else. Parties for all the holidays, other children's birthdays, and important school events (such as celebrating the end of a marking period or the start of summer vacation) feature sugary treats. In her book *Holistic Parenting*, Lynn Wiese Sneyd tells this story in the "food diary" section: "December 3: Last day before Christmas break. Went to Elle's preschool party in the morning. Chamomile tea, apple juice, and cookies without refined sugar, all organic. The kids loved the spread. Went to Hannah's grade school party. Soda, nachos, Cheetos, and sugary, frosted treats. The kids, hyper as could be, loved this spread, too. Felt like I had traveled between two planets but drove no more than 20 miles."

Deal with school parties by bringing small gifts or stickers instead of cupcakes on your child's birthday. Also, have frank talks about sweets with your child's teachers and, especially, with your child.

Traveling and Dining Out

What is it about travel, especially on the road, that makes people eat foods they might never touch at home? Stops en route at convenience stores result in sacks full of cream-filled doughnuts, cheese puffs, ice cream sandwiches, and chartreuse- and purple-colored drinks. (No wonder kids get into such horrendous fights en route.) Amtrak travelers gorge on two or three of the desserts with every dining car meal, and travelers on cruises go quite mad at those dessert buffets, served what seems like every hour all day long.

Your family need not feast on rudeness-causing foods while traveling. Great travel snacks include nuts, apples, oranges, and protein bars. Your child should understand that sugary foods will make her feel awful and ruin her good time. She should stretch her snacks out to every 2 hours, at least, and eat only light meals on the road. Don't think you have to choose only health food places and avoid the more common eateries when traveling. Your child can avoid rudeness-causing foods when eating in fast-food restaurants, if she's willing to make the effort.

I do a lot of bus travel, and buses almost always stop at fast-food places for meals. I order a burger without a bun (I don't eat the bun if the server says the bun must be included), a salad with oil dressing on the side, and mineral water (for drinking later, on the bus), and feel just fine afterward. Yes, it's hard forgoing the fries, milkshakes, and ice cream desserts I see all my fellow travelers gobble up. But then I remember how awful I feel an hour after

(continued on page 164)

Eating Out the Rudeness-Free Way

How do you desensitize your children to the lure of fast-food restaurant meals loaded with carbs, calories, and saturated fats? It's a challenge every parent faces, but solving it successfully is even more critical when you're trying to keep your child from eating foods you suspect make him rude. Check out the following suggestions, which will help you find the healthy choices on any menu.

Give your children a course in fast-food eating. Show them how unhealthful certain fast-food dishes (those with lots of grease, sugar, and refined carbs, such as french fries, bread, and pastry dough) can be. Then explain how much more healthful other fast-food options are, such as crisp, colorful salads (excluding edible tortilla or bread bowls), shimmering soups, carefully cooked veggie side dishes, crispy baked chicken and poached or baked fish entrées unsullied with greasy sauces, and tasty, lean burgers loaded with raw onions, lettuce, and tomato. (Keep in mind that many of these foods, while more healthful than burgers and fries, still contain additives.)

Nutrition guides containing calorie, fat, and carbohydrate information for all menu offerings are available on the Internet for McDonald's, Burger King, Taco Bell, Chick-fil-A, Pizza Hut, and others. To read the nutrition guides, go to your favorite search engine and type in the name of the restaurant plus "Nutrition Guide." Or call the manager of your local fast-food place and ask how you can obtain such a guide. When you get the guide, show your children how some menu choices are healthful and nutritious, while others are loaded with more than a thousand calories and enough saturated fat to cause clogging of the arteries. Children will be interested in these differences.

Make a reservation. When you take your children shopping, decide *en famille* in which healthful food restaurant you will all have lunch or dinner, and make a reservation there as soon as you arrive in the mall. That way, your kids will know they cannot pester you for cookies, chocolates, shakes, and other goodies sold so temptingly in every mall. Besides gaining health benefits, you can save money on buying snacks if you stick to your policy of "No eating till mealtime."

To make your dining-out experience even more enjoyable, keep a copy of the menu at home (most restaurants will be happy to supply you with one). That way, you can have your children decide what they're going to order far ahead of time. This allows you to monitor their choices—and to avoid embarrassing hassles while the server is waiting to take your order.

Teach the art of careful eating in restaurants. Here comes some harsh advice: You should avoid luncheonettes, waffle houses, pancake palaces, and similar kinds of restaurants if you are serious about eliminating rudeness-causing foods. These places are peculiarly American, offering lots of calico on the apple-cheeked waitpersons, gorgeous full-color menus, country-cute decor, and other signifiers of wholesomeness in our culture. But these restaurants make their profits by one main method: serving refined carbs in hundreds of delectable ways, often fried with grease or sweetened with syrup and whipped cream. As lovely as they are to look at, these dishes are just not good for kids. I advise avoiding the temptations of these places altogether.

Careful eating need not mean boring eating, however. It can mean trying new foods from other cultures that are as delicious as they are healthful. Here are some ideas for the more popular ethnic eateries.

(continued)

In Italian restaurants: Avoid high-fat pasta dishes, such as fettuccine Alfredo, lasagna, anything made parmigiana, and all dishes that involve coating the pasta with any kind of oil or fat. Also avoid the antipasto, garlic bread with butter, cream soups, and creamed side dishes. Look instead for entrées featuring plain pasta covered with pure tomato- or meat- or vegetable-based sauces made delicious by spices instead of butter and lard. Also go for clear and thin soups, such as minestrone and soups containing beans. Finally, limit yourself and your kids to one piece each of that terrific Italian bread while waiting for your meals to arrive.

Do teach your kids to enjoy the marsala dishes, chicken cacciatore, cioppino (fish stew), greaseless tomato-based sauces (such as marinara and pizzaolo), and pasta primavera without cream or butter sauce.

Avoid cannelloni, ravioli, or other cheese-filled pasta, any sauce labeled "crema" or "fritto," risotto (a rice dish made with cheese and butter), and veal piccata or saltimbocca.

In Mexican restaurants: Say no to chips, refried beans, fried tortilla bowls, and anything that looks like it might have flour or sugar added. Enjoy plain vegetables, lots of salsa, and guacamole if it hasn't been thickened with flour. Black bean soup, gazpacho, chicken soft tacos, fajitas, seafood prepared Veracruz style (made in herbed tomato sauce), and seviche (fish marinated in lime juice) are terrific. Not great are the chiles rellenos, chimichanga, chorizo, flautas, quesadillas, and taquitos (small fried tacos).

In American steak houses: Encourage your kids to choose sirloin and tenderloin cuts, which are leaner, in the smallest portions available. A 6-ounce portion is considered small in American steak houses, but a 3-ounce portion of red meat is the maximum amount recommended for kids. Avoid all garlic bread, all beans cooked with sugar (such as baked beans) or pork or lard, all stuffed or sour-cream covered baked potatoes, and all salads premade with cream sauce. Allow baked potatoes with a bit of butter or yogurt, plain veggies as side dishes, and salads with dressing on the side.

In Oriental restaurants: Encourage your kids to try hot-and-sour or wonton soup, plain white steamed rice without any type of sauce, shrimp with garlic sauce, Szechuan shrimp, steamed veggies, or stir-fried veggies. Soy dishes are great, as long as they aren't fried. Avoid anything cooked in batter, egg foo yong, egg rolls, fried rice, kung pao chicken, and mu shu pork. Remember, much Chinese and some Japanese food is prepared with sugar, so be on the lookout for a too-sweet taste to ordinary dishes. Also, be sure to ask if the restaurant uses MSG; if it does, ask that your family's meals be prepared without it. Be aware that MSG is particularly common in the soups served in Oriental restaurants.

In Greek restaurants: Go for the fish baked with garlic and tomato sauce (plaki), shish kebab, souvlakia, tabbouleh (bulgur mixed with chopped tomatoes, parsley, mint, olive oil, and lemon juice), torato (a cold soup made with eggplant, peppers, and yogurt), tzatziki (a dip or dressing made with yogurt, garlic, and cucumbers), and avgolemono, a great low-carb broth or dip made from chicken broth, egg yolks, and lemon juice (be aware, though, that the egg yolk content is very high). Avoid baba ghanoush, baklava (too much honey and dough), falafel (deep fried chickpea croquettes), moussaka (meat and eggplant covered with a high-carb béchamel sauce), and spanakopita (vegetable pie with lots of animal fat and dough).

eating those treats (mean, depressed, way too full, and ironically, wanting more fries and shakes right away) and am able to be strong.

I have learned to set my mind on looking forward to enjoying those foods I can eat instead of longing for those I can't, a mental strategy that most parents can easily model and teach to their children.

Restaurants that won't test your child's willpower and will provide him with healthful choices include Mexican, Italian, Asian (especially Japanese, since Chinese food can often be prepared with lots of sugar), and any of those trendy chain establishments, such as Applebee's and Ruby Tuesday's, that offer large salads and lean meats. Steak houses such as Outback are terrific, but a little pricey for many families.

Please, at all costs, avoid buffets. There is no way to prevent kids from overindulging on rudeness-causing foods at these restaurants without creating a memorable horrific scene. I'd also advise against cafeterias or any other place where the kids' choices of food cannot be run past the parents before the order is given. Restaurants reminiscent of ice cream parlors are clearly not a good idea for meals—temptation in the form of huge sundaes and banana splits and milkshakes heaped with whipped cream will abound in colorful pictures on the menus and in real-life versions on other diners' tables. Family restaurants such as JB's and Denny's also feature a few too many gooey dessert photos on the menus to suit me. But they do serve nutritious, rudeness-free foods such as salads and omelettes and lean meats that are good for children and will improve their moods—if you forgo those desserts pictured so temptingly on the menus and the special table cards.

Athletics

What should you give your child before a big sporting event? First of all, sports drinks are loaded with sugar, so I don't recommend them in most cases. And don't think candy bars or sugary drinks will enhance your child's performance on the field or court. They not only won't help, but they'll let him down badly after an hour or so. As his blood sugar level drops, he will most likely feel confused, exhausted, and sleepy and may have a temper tantrum if the match or game isn't going well. Instead, give him a protein bar, which will keep his energy and ability and spirits at a high level.

Drinking lots of water is important, too. Dr. Cabin says that kids involved in endurance and continuous exercises, such as running and cycling, should drink about half a glass of water (about 4 ounces) every 15 to 20 minutes at best and at least every half hour. He believes electrolyte replacement fluids, such as Gatorade, are usually unnecessary because a good diet containing fruits and vegetables will provide all the electrolytes a child needs, and in balance. (The one exception is if your child is involved in endurance events that last longer than 3 hours.) Caffeinated drinks are strictly forbidden, Dr. Cabin warns, because the caffeine acts as a diuretic and the child's body can swiftly become dehydrated as a result.

When it comes to the best diet for an athletic lifestyle, Dr. Cabin has firsthand experience: He's an ardent bicyclist. He says that children who are very athletic—involved in sports that require continuous effort several times a week, such as basketball and track—should eat many more carbs than sedentary kids because exercising, especially doing endurance activities, uses more complex carbs for fuel than does sitting, sleeping, and playing video games.

If your child is very athletic, make sure that half of what he eats consists of complex carbs. If his caloric allotment is, say, 3,000 calories a day, then 1,500 of those calories should be provided by potatoes, whole wheat grain, vegetables, and fruit. He should not rely on refined sugar and flour products to get his carbs or think that he can eat these no-no foods freely because he's so active. These foods can hurt his performance and health because the energy they provide is too brief in duration, and the letdown when that energy runs out is too dramatically sudden. A child who regularly eats refined carbs during sports will feel not so much angry and aggressive (which might be great for some competitive sports!) but more confused and discouraged and hopeless—none of which will help him achieve his best athletic performance.

Please, begs Dr. Cabin, don't let your child participate in such sports as gymnastics or wrestling if the coaches enforce weight limits. Losing lots of weight quickly before an event can severely reduce the health and performance of the young athlete.

Watching TV

America's habit of eating while viewing has become so ingrained that it's almost impossible to break. And most of the foods desired during viewing are rudeness-causing to the extreme—chips and candy and ice cream, washed down by liters of soda, usually containing sugar and caffeine. All you can do in this problem situation is substitute foods you want your kids to eat for the foods you don't want them to have and limit quantities. Fresh fruit cut up and speared with wooden picks, celery spread with almond butter, mixed nuts, and dry-roasted soy nuts are all good options.

Here are some rules that will help limit snacking during TV-watching and turn it into as healthy an activity as possible. First, some definite don'ts:

- No eating out of the bag or can or package. This promotes excessive snacking and the notion that your children can just eat until the bag is empty.
- No begging for seconds on servings of snacks. One serving is it.
- No sneaking bites to or from other members of your household, especially from unsuspecting younger siblings.

And now for some do's:

- Snacks must be eaten from bowls or dishes.
- No TV during meals—even if that's when you like to catch up on the news. When you eat, stay focused on the food you're eating and each other's company.
- Use dinnertime to discuss important family issues, news events, even the TV shows your children watch. This teaches your kids to express their opinions and shows them their opinions are valued.
- Exercise while watching TV. Try an age-appropriate activity such as running on a treadmill, doing calisthenics, or riding an exercise bicycle. (Just make sure the bike doesn't have spoked wheels, which could injure a young child.) Join in on the fun, and you'll all enjoy the benefits of family-centered exercise.

Visiting Friends and Relatives

Oh, the relatives. They're almost certain to be your worst nemesis when you're trying to change your family's diet to rudeness-free foods. There is usually one person in every family who acts as the boss of everybody, and her word—especially her word on nutrition—is law. If she happens to believe (as our family matriarch, my mother's mother, did) that inch-thick lumpy flapjacks covered with imitation maple syrup and finished off with a plateful of full-fat vanilla ice cream is the best meal a child can eat because it "sticks to his little ribs and he eats every bite," you're in for an interesting experience. You have to find a way to praise her cooking and yet avoid eating at her house. Or having her cook at yours.

I've found that the best way to do this is to be evasive, finding reasons why "coming over for supper" is just not possible today. Teach your children to be polite to this person, but to say they "just ate" if offered any food. And be sure to always visit this person in between meal times.

Some families are highly offended if you don't eat second or third helpings of all food served. Children should be instructed to eat a little of their second portion, if they cannot get out of accepting it, and then very graciously say they are full. Instead of consuming snacks and sugared drinks at these homes in order to be polite, your kids should be able to say they have a problem with certain foods and ask for ice water and a piece of fruit instead. Or they can take out one of their own snacks to eat. Think your kids will never have such self-control? Oh, but they will, by the time you change their thinking by implementing all the advice in this book!

making it happen

Nice book, you're probably thinking at this point.

For someone else's family.

Your family is never together long enough for you to even discuss a new diet regimen, much less implement it. Your older kids have jobs and sports practice after school and on weekends, and they live on a diet of fast-food burgers, microwave pizza, and Hot Pockets, eaten on the run with diet Coke and fruit-flavored drinks dyed blue and orange. Your younger child spends most of her time with a babysitter or your parents—who feed her a steady diet of fried food, hot dogs, and sweets. You and the kids never have meals together, except maybe for Sunday dinner, which is often eaten at the kids' favorite buffet place. Actually, that's kind of a relief. The kids can get so rude and sullen when they're with you they set your nerves on edge.

Or maybe it's your spouse who's the problem, complaining if you serve anything but meat, potatoes, and apple pie. He or she is unwilling to help convince your children to eat other types of food—but blames you when the kids get out of control or get into problems at school.

I hope it's not all as bad as that for you. But, judging from the parents whom I've met, it often is that bad—and worse. In a recent *Wall Street Journal* article on kids and food, Kelly Stitt, a senior brand manager in charge of EZ Squirt ketchup for Heinz, reported that "Kids want to feel like they're in control of everything, including mealtime." So far, Stitt added, parents are giving kids whatever they want in the supermarket. That's because parents, especially working parents, refuse to spend what little time they have together with their children arguing about food. Sound familiar?

The problem, says Dr. Cabin, is that parents think the food kids want is what's best for them. In reality, the foods kids like best are often the foods that make them feel and behave the worst. The good news is that by changing your children's eating habits using the strategies outlined in this book, you can stop your kids' rudeness, and their demands for unhealthful foods, in as little as 1 week. In the process, you'll be improving their health and the happiness of your home. Here are smart ways to make changes that increase children's respect for food and also will improve your communication with your children dramatically. If you have virtually no communication with them at all (don't worry, you're not alone), you will soon.

Present the Plan

It's important to tell your family members that you want to make food changes for their good and to give them some idea of what's in store. This helps get their attention and helps you keep your commitment to following through on your changes. You can't get the kids to stay in one place long enough to tell them anything? Write them a letter! Mail it to them, if necessary.

If you can't think of what to say in your letter, customize this letter and sign your name.

My dear children:
I've been reading about nutrition. I want to change our eating habits because I want you to look and feel your best. I want you to be able to reach your potential in life.

The kinds of foods we've been eating have been causing problems. They make us grouchy and irritable because they don't give our bodies what we need to grow and stay healthy.

The kinds of food I'm going to provide will make you feel and look terrific and perhaps even lose weight.

Here, to get it over with, is the bad news about these food changes.

- Your tastebuds are going to love our new way of eating, but maybe not right away. It might take a little time to get used to it.
- We're going to watch how much we eat—no more eating and snacking all night long.
- You won't be eating all of the same foods that your friends eat. But you'll feel better, and I think pretty soon they'll notice and want to try the food that you're eating.
- You may feel hungry at times, especially early on. But don't worry. You will be getting plenty to eat. And that hungry feeling won't last.

Here's the good news.
- This way of eating is cool. Celebrities, movie stars, and models use it.

- *This way of eating will save you money that you can use for other things like clothes and movies.*
- *You'll have more energy and be less stressed out.*
- *You'll do better in school.*

Here's my schedule for implementing these food changes.

1. *We'll have a meeting on ___ at ___ a.m.*
   (I've found that morning works best for these.)
2. *At that time, I'll give you individualized food plans with the amount of calories and protein you can have every day.*
3. *We'll decide then which days we'll all eat dinner together.*
4. *I'll answer any questions you might have.*

Love, Mom (and/or Dad)

If you feel silly communicating with your children in such a formal way, be assured that this kind of communication is exactly what they need and want. And they must have it to stay the course in the face of peer pressure.

During the meeting, follow these tips for the best results.

- Be honest. Tell your children that from their behavior, you have begun to suspect they don't feel all that well. Add that if they stick to the food rules you give them, they should start feeling better in about a week—better than they ever knew they could feel.
- Present the rules in a no-nonsense way.
- Do provide reading material that makes your food changes seem classy and positive. Look for health-conscious models, musicians, and athletes who talk about the importance of eating well and staying active.

After you've explained the changes, follow through on your stated intentions. Yes, you'll get protests and cries of "I'm not doing this!" Ignore these complaints. You can, contrary to messages given to moms and dads in our child-centered culture, decide what's best for your children and follow through on it.

Your spouse, of course, may be a different matter. If he (or she) won't cooperate, let him eat his usual diet. Pretty soon that kind of food will seem heavy, out of date, and not appealing at all.

If your children are young, you have little to worry about. Young children love to be guided in their activities by parents who love them. You may get some resistance over stopping the flow of candy, but their behavior will improve so much that you'll be able to manage these squabbles without the tantrums of the past.

Guidelines for Implementing Change

Here are some guidelines you'll want to use from the start.

- Be a micromanager about your children's food intake. Decide what, when, and where it's okay to eat. For instance, forbid eating in the car and bedrooms.
- Stick to the portions specified in your individual food plan.
- Don't give up on your new eating plan. Your family will try to test your resolve almost daily, because no one likes changes.
- Don't let hunger strikes deter you. Sooner or later, your children will join you. And when they do, they'll be set for a healthier and happier life.

When it comes to the food that is brought into your house and the preparation of it, follow these tips.

- Throw out contraband food found stashed in kids' rooms. This is your house. You can get rid of foods you don't want in it.

(continued on page 178)

DR. CABIN'S
Nutritional Breakthroughs

Trapped in a Vicious Circle of Destructive Behavior:

Alberta's Story

There's no question that changing your family's diet will sometimes be a struggle. In fact, it no doubt will lead to some unpleasant scenes in the beginning, when your children aren't yet used to the changes and put up a fuss. But don't despair: In the long run, the positive effects of eating nourishing, health-promoting food will more than make up for the little bit of discomfort your kids may feel now.

One particularly sad case that haunts Dr. Cabin is that of Alberta. While her story doesn't have a happy ending, Dr. Cabin believes it's an important cautionary tale for those times when giving in to your children's pleas for processed, sugary foods seems so tempting.

Alberta had severe behavioral problems that had been escalating since she was an infant. Physicians her family had consulted had been unable to figure out what was wrong and either suggested prescription drugs or predicted that she would grow out of these behaviors. But she didn't grow out of the behaviors and drugs were not an option that Alberta's family wanted to try.

By the time she was 5 years old, Alberta was having tantrums several times a day, was angry at everyone, including her kindergarten teachers, and would not concentrate on lessons for any length of time. Her single dad, who was the custodial parent, was beside himself with worry. So was Alberta's grandmother, who was helping to raise her. The dad then heard about Dr. Cabin and took Alberta to see him.

Dr. Cabin suspected food allergies and gave Alberta the appropriate tests. The results showed she was so allergic to some foods, such as fish, corn, peanuts, tomatoes, and dairy foods, that she was in danger of going into anaphylactic shock (a potentially fatal condition) just from smelling them cooking. In addition, she was so sensitive to sugar, food dyes, food preservatives, and wheat that her behavior and concentration became uncontrollable when she ate these foods.

Once her diet was adjusted so that these foods and food additives were eliminated, Alberta's behavior improved dramatically. She made friends, enjoyed school, and was a responsible, delightful daughter to her dad and grandmother. She continued to see Dr. Cabin two or three times a year, so that she could have her medical condition checked and her tests repeated. Her father and grandmother were delighted with her physical, emotional, and academic progress.

(continued)

Unfortunately, upon turning 16, Alberta decided she could choose what she ate. She believed that not sharing her friends' eating experiences was seriously impairing her social life. She was getting a reputation as weird and was feeling left out. She had a right to have fun just like everyone else!

Her dad and grandmother tried to get her to remain on the diet Dr. Cabin recommended, but with only limited success. While Alberta agreed to continue avoiding the foods to which she was extremely allergic, she announced that she was now going to eat everything else her teen friends ate, such as pizza, soda, "DQ" (Dairy Queen treats), "Micky D's" (McDonald's food), and "BK" (Burger King cuisine). No, she would not consult Dr. Cabin before going off her diet. After all, Alberta reasoned, she knew more about her body than he did and was sure she had outgrown her inability to tolerate these foods. If she was still affected by these foods, well, no problem. She had enough self-control to handle any difficult reactions they caused.

After just a week or so of taking charge of her own diet, Alberta had lost control of her life. Not only had she reverted to the hostile behavior and unwillingness to concentrate in school that she had shown before going on Dr. Cabin's diet, but she had also taken up new behaviors such as smoking, drinking alcohol, and using recreational drugs. She was asked to leave school because of her difficult behavior in class and inability to concentrate and was put in an alternative, less-structured high school—which she seldom bothers to attend. On Alberta's next visit to Dr. Cabin, which was about 3 months ago as of this writing, she admitted to him that she was headed for trouble and promised to return to her former diet. Unfortunately, she didn't keep her promise.

Alberta's father recently reported to Dr. Cabin that Alberta has graduated to petty crime and is now on probation for shoplifting. Dr. Cabin wasn't surprised at this report. He says that her poor diet could cause her to have not only hostile, angry feelings and a lack of emotional control, but cravings. He notes that cravings for certain foods (often for the foods to which the person is allergic) are often a symptom of food allergies. These cravings can escalate to the point where they include cravings for alcohol, drugs, and exhilarating experiences (such as the thrill of shoplifting) that can result in addictions to these substances and experiences. Alberta is obviously suffering such cravings and will continue to do so and to be unable to control her angry behavior until she herself decides to do what's best for her health and return to her former diet.

- Involve your kids in food preparation. Don't require that they help, but do invite them to create the salad or help you wash some veggies. If they're old enough to use a knife, they can also help chop veggies.
- Please, please avoid candy, soda, cake, chips, cookies, and anything else with sugar in it.
- Do provide healthful snacks at all times. Allow your kids to enjoy a snack every 2½ hours.

In addition to the new food regimen, you will want to institute new policies on family exercise. Try these ideas.

- Make exercise a family thing. Enroll in a gym that can accommodate kids or have a personal trainer visit your family once a week and give group and individual instruction to you and your kids.
- Set exercise goals for every child (running is easy to do and easy to keep track of). Offer rewards for kids who reach their goals.
- Buy some fun and inexpensive exercise equipment that can be used in front of the television. If you use them yourself, the children will, too.

If the ideas above seem too structured, consider this truth: Your family, and you as their leader, can benefit greatly from a more structured guidance. If you really want results, you have to acknowledge that they won't just happen by accident. You have to establish the structure that will enable success.

Practical Tips from Experts

Here are some valuable tips from experts on kids' nutrition.

Don't force, but do finish. If your child complains about what's served for dinner, tell her she doesn't have to eat it, recommends

Nancy Ann Schwartz, R.N., of Searchlight, a private medical consulting firm in Orange, California. "Do not offer to fix her what she wants," Schwartz continues. "She'll almost always return to the table after 20 minutes or so and enjoy the meal that is served. Don't, however, wait too long for her to come back and eat. When you finish your meal, that's it. Tell her that the kitchen is closed." Yes, she may have to go to bed hungry that night, but she'll never wait too long to come back to the table again!

Call the shots. "Don't say such things as, 'My children won't drink milk unless I put chocolate in it,'" Schwartz advises. "That's letting your kids be the bosses of you. Simply don't allow chocolate syrup in your house."

Love to cook. Learn to love cooking, no matter how old you are, says Lynn Wiese-Sneyd. In her book, *Holistic Parenting*, she tells how she learned to cook well by trial and error and learning from many culinary "flops." "There's no way around this one," she writes. "You have to learn to cook. It's how fresh and healthful food gets prepared."

She also says that the eating of food should be made into a spiritual experience. Turn off the TV, don't answer phone calls, and make sure there is a sense of communing and sharing, she stresses. The conversation should include discussion of the day's events for all family members present. By doing this, you'll make mealtime a joyful experience your kids will remember the rest of their lives.

When necessary, try some scare tactics. As a last resort, you can always try scaring your kids into adopting your food changes by telling them about diabetes—a disease caused by too much sugar and refined carbohydrates that can lead to blindness, amputations, and kidney failure, among other devastating effects. You could also mention the painful daily shots of insulin that are necessary for people with type 1 diabetes and are often needed by people with type 2. "Few people, especially children, realize how miserable diabetes can be," says Catherine Robinson, R.D., a diabetes educator for three hospitals in Arizona who sees its debilitating effects every day.

The incidence of type 2 diabetes (the kind caused by obesity and an insulin-producing diet) has risen alarmingly in children, a result of changes in the American diet and an accompanying drop in exercise levels. The biggest risk factor for the condition is being overweight.

Robinson believes that the increase in teen's sugar consumption is largely to blame. Because of this alarming trend, she thinks kids are better off learning to get along without sugar. "Instead of recommending alternative sweeteners, I tell my clients not to cater to their sweet tooth at all," she says. "Learning to eat and drink things that are not sweet is hard to get used to, but it certainly can be done," Robinson adds. And kids must understand that type 2 diabetes can be prevented by the kinds of changes in diet and exercise you want them to make.

How do you find information for kids on type 2 diabetes? Call your local hospital and ask if there are any diabetes education programs in your town. You may be able to get a diabetes educator to present a special program to your kids and a few of their friends and their parents. The American Diabetes Association is also a rich source of information and help; they can be reached through their Web site at www.diabetes.org.

If your children are overweight at all, they should be checked for type 2 diabetes frequently, Robinson and Dr. Cabin both warn. "Too many people wait until real symptoms, such as blurred vision and neuropathy (loss of feeling in the limbs), set in," Robinson adds. "By then, drastic measures must be taken, or kidney and heart disease—heart disease is a much more common result of diabetes than people realize—and other debilitating conditions could be imminent."

You Are Not Alone: Parents' Stories

If you talk to other parents, you begin to see that you are not alone. Many families have problems with rudeness-causing foods. Their experiences will help you realize you're not imagining things with your own kids.

Most of the stories I hear deal with the same culprits—foods containing caffeine, sugar, or food dyes. You'll also notice that sometimes the biggest challenge in these situations is convincing other adults in the family of the problem!

• Child-care director Jennifer Leacock noticed that her 3-year-old, Thomas, would become really difficult after eating ketchup. "He would pour half the bottle onto his food, then eat the ketchup and get so antsy. His behavior would become obstinate. And he wouldn't eat anything else. Dinner was ruined for him—and, usually, everyone eating with him." She doesn't let him have ketchup at dinner anymore, and now he's a much more pleasant dinner companion. But because of her work hours, Jennifer's mom often takes Thomas out to dinner, where he demands ketchup and sugary foods. Jennifer is now trying to get her mom not to give Thomas these foods, "but my mom thinks kids should have whatever they want to eat!" she says.

• A bank employee, who preferred to remain anonymous (I'll call him Walter), says he thinks his daughter's day-care provider is loading the child with sweets all day. What makes matters worse is that the day-care provider is also Walter's mother-in-law! "When we

(continued on page 184)

ASK DR. CABIN ?? ???????????

Q. *What's the difference between children who eat too many refined carbs and become rude and children with diabetes?*

A. A child who becomes rude after eating too many refined carbs can still be basically healthy. The carbs can cause the child's blood sugar level to temporarily rise and then drop very dramatically. She could then behave very rudely and feel very miserable. It's been my experience that the amount of refined carbs necessary to produce this reaction varies with the individual child. Sometimes a child can go for years gorging on refined carbs and be fine; other times, one or two servings can produce the rude behavior. Some children can gorge on refined carbs their entire lives and never get rude. It just depends on the individual metabolism.

Children who have diabetes have a physical condition or illness that is not going to go away unless treated. The causes of diabetes aren't completely known, but genetics and factors such as obesity and lack of exercise appear to be involved. Type 1 diabetes usually occurs in people under 30 years of age and appears suddenly. Genetics is usually involved.

Type 2 diabetes can be caused by genetics or obesity brought on by a diet of too much sugar and refined carbs coupled with a lack of exercise. Cases of type 2 diabetes have tripled in the general population since 1990. With type 2 diabetes, either the body becomes resistant to the action of insulin, or glucose has trouble entering the cells because the pancreas can't produce enough insulin. As a result, blood sugar levels rise to dangerous levels, leading to all kinds of degenerative conditions, including kidney failure, deterioration of the eye that could result in blindness, progressive nerve damage and blockage of the blood vessels that can result in circulation so poor that it can even become necessary to amputate the toes and feet, intestinal problems, and fungal (yeast) infections such as ringworm, vaginitis, and athlete's foot.

Q. *So a child with undiagnosed diabetes may never get food-induced rudeness?*

A. A child who has diabetes may never feel mean or rude or enraged as a result of the foods he eats. In fact, I've found that he may have no outward symptoms of his condition for years. Eventually, however, he can get lots of other symptoms besides rudeness that are pretty awful, especially in childhood and adolescence, when feeling and looking his best are so important. These symptoms include feeling chronically tired and slowed down. He may also feel a constant state of anxiety about his frequent need to urinate, constant need to eat, inability to stop gaining weight, and his desire to sleep a lot of the time.

Q. *Are blood tests the only way to check if a child has diabetes?*

A. They are the only sure way. But I urge the parents of my young patients not to wait until the blood test results are in to limit the child's refined carbs and get him on regular daily exercise. Both of these strategies have been found to reverse type 2 diabetes in some kids and keep them from having to take insulin by injection.

pick up our little girl after work, she's so wired. She's mean and hard to control for hours." But, he added, "On the weekends, when we don't let her have that kind of food, she settles down and is nice as can be." Walter said he and his wife are trying to figure out how to have a talk with his mother-in-law, but can't quite determine the best way to do it.

• Another mother, Pat Varney, said her daughter was so mean to her that Pat actually had to send her to live with her dad. The girl later gave up all sweets in order to clear up her complexion, and the turnaround was remarkable. "Now, she's very, very nice to me, her mother," Pat says with a chuckle. "Really, I couldn't ask for a nicer daughter than the one I have now."

Making the Organic Choice

Now that you are on the road to giving your children the most healthful diet possible, it's time to take a close look at the role organic foods should play in your meal plan. Is organic food really better for your kids than other food? More and more parents, educators, and scientists are beginning to believe that it is. Dr. Cabin, for one, is a firm believer that in many cases, organic foods can improve your child's behavior. "Organic foods are much less likely to contain the antibiotics, steroids, hormones, and food dyes that can have negative effects on the way kids feel and act," he explains.

He's not alone in advocating organics:

• Diana Erney, senior research associate of Rodale's *OG*, America's leading publication on organic gardening, has observed a genuine concern that the pesticides and chemicals often used on nonorganic produce may be associated with learning disabilities in kids.

- Among the evidence of this link is a report from the Environmental Working Group (EWG) that explains that the faster metabolism in children and lack of a blood brain barrier in infants make youngsters' brains vulnerable to the harmful effects of chemicals. It goes on to say that youngsters who are affected by these chemicals are less able to learn.
- According to a report by the Mount Sinai School of Medicine, because children have higher metabolic rates than adults—and different detoxification processes and body compositions—they absorb chemicals in their food more quickly.
- Chemicals (such as those found in pesticide residues on food) that may not be too harmful to adults were found by the National Academy of Science to be 10 times more toxic to infants and children, whose developing brains are especially vulnerable to their effects.

Buying Organic

There are two important facts you need to understand about buying organic food. The first is that not all of it is as attractive as nonorganic produce. That's because organic food contains none of the dyes and shine-producing chemicals that make nonorganic produce—especially apples and oranges—look so enticing. The second thing is that you may have to shop for produce more frequently. Organic produce has fewer preserving chemicals and does not stay fresh as long as nonorganic produce that has been bred for long-distance shipping. To be on the safe side, organic produce should be used within 3 days after purchase, Dr. Cabin recommends.

Once you have your food plans set for your kids, make your shopping list. If you don't have a natural foods market near your home, try to find organic food sections in your supermarket's produce department. In some areas of the country, people form cooperatives for buying organic foods directly from the farmers who grow them. Mail-order sources for food and other organic products are also plentiful. One very useful Web site for locating organics is offered by Rodale's *Organic Style* magazine and can be found at www.organicstyle.com.

If you are unable to find organic food, buy regular produce in your supermarket and wash it carefully.

In addition to his recommendations for buying fresh, organic produce, Dr. Cabin also advises looking for certified organic poultry, eggs, dairy products, and beef, which are produced from animals raised on organic grain and are hormone-free. "Beef and poultry that are organically fed and hormone-free are going to be free of chemicals that have been shown to damage the immune systems of children and affect their behavior," says Dr. Cabin. "And organic dairy products don't harbor the hormones and antibiotics that are harmful to children." Eggs should be from chickens that are hormone-free. You may also want to look for eggs and chicken that are labeled "free range" or "cage-free," which indicates they are allowed to move around a little and eat on their own. (Believe me, if you ever found out how commercial chickens are treated and fed, you'd never touch another one in your life, let alone feed them to your kids.)

Note that some brands of eggs and meat will be labeled as hormone-free or antibiotic-free, but not be certified organic because they haven't been fed exclusively on organic grain. That's still a big improvement over conventionally raised products, so you can feel good about buying these products for your family.

While there is not yet organic certification for fish, look for smaller fish such as trout and Alaskan salmon (avoid farm-raised fish, which are subject to antibiotic treatments), advises Dr. Cabin. The larger fish, such as tuna and swordfish, have been shown to contain too much mercury, PCBs, and other chemicals for children's health.

Finally, be aware that even organic food needs to be thoroughly washed, preferably in filtered water. Dr. Cabin says that lead, arsenic, chlorine, and other chemicals found in much of the drinking water today could leech into your food as it soaks in the water. The cheapest pitcher filters are fine for filtering most drinking water.

Soak the produce and keep emptying the soaking water until the water is clear of all soil. Scrub potatoes and cut out all sprouts. Peel nonorganic apples, since the skin absorbs most of the pesticides. OG's Diana Erney reports she's found washing produce with plenty of good, clean water to be just as good as using the specialty produce-washing products that are currently on the market.

Cooking Up Good Health

For the health and happiness of your family, it's essential to shun processed foods as much as possible and instead cook fresh foods from scratch. Any food that has been processed and packaged into a prepared side dish or entrée loses some of its nutrients. It also is usually loaded with carbs, sugar, chemicals, and dyes, all of which can cause the behavioral problems we've discussed.

Further, eating processed foods "enriched" with vitamins is not as good as getting natural vitamins from fresh foods that are "live," stresses Dr. Cabin. In fact, eating enriched foods can actually lead to overdosing on certain vitamins, such as vitamins A and D, and minerals, such as zinc, that can be toxic in large amounts, especially to children. And when the quality of the added vitamins is inferior and the amounts are over the daily limit or occur in unbalanced combinations, the enriched products can be worse for the child than products that haven't been enriched.

Be sure to involve your children in the process of cooking fresh meals from scratch. Children need to learn how to do this kind of cooking themselves, and watching you do it is one of the best ways for them to pick up the necessary skills. Fortunately, cooking from scratch doesn't have to mean hours spent slaving in the kitchen. Here are some tips to make cooking healthful meals as quick and easy as possible.

- If you don't have the time to buy and cook meat, buy pre-cooked organic meat or fish at your deli. Then just slice it or chop it for meat entrées, soup, omelettes, rolling up with veggie fillings, or mixing with mayo and celery for chicken salad.
- Buy a large, clear plastic or glass bowl. Layer in salad ingredients, including lettuce and a range of colorful veggies, then serve without tossing. The layers will be visible and look like a delicious, colorful torte.
- When you're rushed for time, use liquid egg whites for omelettes. They're faster to use than powdered egg whites because they don't have to be beaten. Don't get in the habit of using these too often, though, since organic versions of these products are not widely available.
- Try a low-carb pancake mix for creating more healthful pancakes and other pastrylike foods. These taste like flour-based mixes, but they won't upset your kids' blood sugar levels or trigger rudeness attacks. Just be sure to check the label and

avoid products that contain sweeteners that might rouse your kids' desires for real sugar again. Also, don't let your kids load up the pancakes with sugary syrups; instead use fruit in its natural juices.

- When you know your schedule will be busy, work ahead. Prepare a couple days' worth of salads and vegetable dishes ahead of time. Wash and cut up meat for easy cooking. Put breakfast foods all in one place so you can fix that meal in a few minutes every morning. Put lunch and snack foods in another spot.

- Teach the kids to make at least one meal, side dish, or dessert each week. Help them make a hearty stew, a crustless quiche or frittata, or a sugarless cheesecake. Make cooking and eating healthfully a family activity you do together.

- Master the fundamentals of cooking with live foods in the amounts your family members are allowed to eat. Then let your creativity soar. Read cookbooks regularly (and let your kids read along) to find recipes you can adapt to your food plan.

- Keep your best recipe creations and adaptations in an envelope for sharing with other parents who tell you, "I want to change my family's food plan, too—but I have no idea where to start!"

- When you can't find the time to cook, try an occasional frozen, microwave-ready dish made from organic ingredients. Health food stores and natural foods supermarkets have a surprisingly wide variety of dishes from which to choose.

11

your new happy home: making positive changes that last

Creating and maintaining a happy home is more than just making sure your kids eat right. To make really lasting changes and meaningful progress, you need to think of your home life in broad terms.

As we saw in earlier chapters, your body is a network of different systems working together, and your diet is a combination of many different kinds of nutrients working together. In the same way, your home is a combination of many factors that bring joy. Ending rudeness, for instance, certainly helps. But what if other problems persist? What if family members remain uncommunicative, all going their separate ways? What if you succeed in making some changes to your child's diet, but keep on eating poorly yourself? What if you can't muster the self-discipline to stay consistent with your changes in the face of your child's resistance?

What if, in your zeal to change your family's diet, you alienate them? What if you don't show love and affection for your family members that lets them know you want what's best for them, not just what's convenient for you?

Many factors work together, synergistically, to make the home happy. Changing your family's diet has to be integrated into your home life, not just imposed on it as yet another rule of the house. It's easy to see that in order to establish lasting peace in your household, you'll need a plan that is geared toward more than just counting calories and eliminating offending foods.

Happily, there is such a plan!

Designed by Robert E. Calmes, Ed.D., this behavioral plan involves the simultaneous, interactive use of six factors known to be most important to a happy home. Dr. Calmes, professor emeritus in educational psychology at the University of Arizona in Tucson, isolated these factors from more than 2,000 studies of both successful and troubled families. Following are these six characteristics, along with ways you can incorporate them into your family's life.

Modeling by the adults in the home of the behavior and attitudes they want the children to adopt. If, for instance, you want your children to be polite and considerate, then you must treat all family members with politeness and consideration. This is a simple idea, but one that is too often neglected by busy, stressed parents. It's easy to fall into the trap of bossing your child around to get him to act quickly and without discussion. Yet it could be that same tone that he picks up on when *he* wants something and tries to boss *you* around.

Reinforcement of desired behavior. Too often, we lose sight of the fact that kids need reinforcement—or, as Dr. Calmes puts it, "more praise than blame, more reward than punishment." When you see your child acting or speaking in a way that you approve of, tell her so.

Consistency in parental behavior and attitudes. Nothing can undermine children's self-esteem faster than having adults be nice one day and cold or distant or mean the next, without giving any reason for the change. Being consistent does not mean, Dr. Calmes emphasizes, that you can't make a mistake now and then, such as yelling when you don't mean to or letting your guard down in some other way. But it does mean that you have to acknowledge these lapses to your kids, and let them know you didn't mean to do or say what you did.

For good mental health, a child needs to be able to count on consistent attitudes in the adults who take care of him. "That's why some children are mentally healthy despite having abusive and neglectful parents," Dr. Calmes adds. "At least those parents were consistent in their bad parenting—and the child could work with that consistency, negative as it was, to separate himself from them emotionally and maybe even physically at an early age."

Adults who provide rational reasons for their beliefs, standards, and behaviors. Children are not born knowing why they should do some things and not others; they need parents who will explain these reasons. You need not, and should not, explain your reasons more than once, Dr. Calmes says. If the child tells you later that he didn't hear your explanation (meaning he wasn't paying attention), say calmly, "I'm sorry. I hope you listen the next time I explain my reasons to you."

Adults who show empathic understanding of other family members. Try to remember what it was like to be a child. Show your child that you understand how hard it is to deal with bullies, or mean teachers, or objects of crushes who don't reciprocate your feelings, or any of the other overwhelming problems that kids can face. The trick here is to let your child vent his feelings but not give in to self-pity. He needs to feel that he has your admiration for showing grace under pressure, but not your encouragement to become a wimp.

The best way to help your child cope with his problems once you've shown empathy for his distress is by asking these kinds of questions: "Do you have any ideas abut how you can deal with this problem? What are the things you can do now, or tomorrow, that might help?" If he can't suggest any solutions, you can come up with a few ideas. If he suggests a solution that's inappropriate, explain why it might not work and ask him for some other ideas. In other words, encourage problem-solving instead of worrying.

Genuine care and concern for all animals, plants, persons, and things. This means showing loving care of pets, plants, and people in the family (including those with disabilities and who live alone and are lonely) as well as of property. Why property? Because property that is valuable to other members of the family should be respected, says Dr. Calmes.

Families who show this genuine care and concern can be happy in reduced, even impoverished, circumstances. That's because all members, including kids, know how to love and value what they do have instead of longing for what they don't have.

Interestingly, separate studies by such organizations as the Partnership for a Drug-Free America and the National Institute for Drug Abuse (NIDA) have shown many of these factors, especially those dealing with consistency and communication, to be strong protective factors in preventing substance abuse in children. Dr. Calmes says that the families who practice these factors are not necessarily blissfully happy all the time—they can still have their problems. But they are much better able to deal with problems than families who do not demonstrate the six factors.

In addition, families with these factors are more content on a day-to-day basis because members tend to be tightly bonded and loving and because their home is the place where they love to be. These six factors are especially powerful during times of major change instituted by the parents in the family's values and behavior—such as modifying the family's eating habits.

The Calmes Plan provides a framework you can use in every aspect of guiding your family. You'll find the plan particularly useful when you institute changes to your family's diet, since it will enable you to introduce the changes with respect for your child, yet a firm resolve to make the changes stick.

Incorporating the "AAA" Method into the Calmes Plan

The Calmes Plan is for everyday family life with kids. The "AAA" method outlined in chapter 7 is for dealing with specific incidents of rudeness from kids. Here is an example of the ways in which these plans are synergistic.

The "Acknowledge" step shows consistency of parental behavior as well as concern for people in the family. When you observe rude behavior, you consistently point it out to your child and express your disapproval. You inform her that her actions are not acceptable in your family and that they harm the spirit of genuine care and concern for family members. "Sydney, rolling your eyes and calling me a stupid jerk is unacceptable." That's all you have to say. Sydney will get the idea.

The "Announce" step allows you to communicate a rational reason why you will do something—or in this case, not do something—as a result of the rude speech. "Because of your rudeness, Sydney, I am not going to drive you to soccer practice today."

The "Act" step shows consistency of parental behavior and attitude. You act immediately to deal with the rude person and preserve the happiness of the family. Acting in this case means not taking Sydney to soccer practice—despite her insistence that missing this practice will render her ineligible for the next big game, get her thrown off the team, cause her team members to hate her, and make her life miserable in other ways. This acting on your part shows that you put the family's welfare before that of the soccer team, which is exactly what you *should* do.

If Sydney's rudeness continues beyond this incident, despite repeated use of the AAA method, she might indeed be suffering from food-induced rudeness. Check out her diet at once!

Applying the Calmes Plan to Food Changes

Making changes in your family's everyday dietary habits is the perfect opportunity to practice the six factors of Dr. Calmes's plan in your home. Using the plan as a guide, here's how you can ensure that the changes you make are permanent and accepted respectfully by your children.

1. *Model* **the dietary changes yourself.** Don't expect your kids to forgo rudeness-inducing foods while you consume fancy flavored coffee, gourmet ice cream, or cream-filled doughnuts just like you've done for years. At least one parent has to appear to embrace the new food regimen with gusto and make the changes along with your child.

Talk about the food, the cooking, the recipes. For example, savor the salads at family meals; praise the deliciousness of the fresh tomato and green pepper. You should be seen reading appropriate cookbooks in your spare time, signaling how important this new way of eating is to your family. You can bring your child along with you on field trips to farmers' markets and ethnic groceries that stock fresh, healthful foods such as those from Italy and Greece.

Don't restrict your modeling of behavior to food. Get your children involved in other evening activities besides snacking. After dinner, say, "Now it's time to work on photo mobiles (or some other craft project) for this year's Christmas presents." Then set up the card table and craft projects in the living room—yes, you'll be competing with the TV, but that's good. Don't allow the children to retreat to their rooms except for homework and sleep. Keep TV-watching to a minimum, if you can—far too much of the food advertised on commercials is the kind that sets up cravings and makes kids really rude.

2. *Reinforce* your child's adoption of the dietary changes. When your child helps in any way with food preparation, thank him and congratulate him. If he shows any willingness at all, with or without enthusiasm, to eat the new food, tell him how wonderful he is for being so open-minded and how happy it makes you feel to see him eat what you know will make him look and feel his best.

Buy him a cool new lunch box that he can use to carry his new, nutritious lunches. Talk about food with him, discussing every detail, such as the differences between cilantro and parsley. Praise his considered opinions on the subject and his ability to state his case. Boast to your spouse or parents, when your child can hear you, about what a healthy eater he is becoming.

3. *Show consistency* in serving and eating the new foods. This means, simply, not submitting to pleas to go to Burger King "just this once" or order in pizza and fried bread "because I got an A on the math test." All you have to say is, "Sweetheart, we don't eat that way now." Then suggest a different way to celebrate, like renting a video game, playing miniature golf, or going swimming at the Y. Giving in to "just this once" pleas amounts to being inconsistent and sends the wrong message to your child—that breaking your food rules is a way to celebrate. The food changes you're making are for every day, not just some days. And you certainly don't want the forbidden foods to become a kind of reward for achievement— that's completely backward.

If your child insists on a food treat, suggest that you purchase a pizza with organic ingredients from the natural foods super-market, or make yogurt sundaes with raspberries sweetened with stevia. And by all means, do not accommodate your kids' friends "who don't eat food like this." The children's dinner guests eat what your family eats—it's as simple as that. Your own child may be surprised to learn that his guest has never tried a certain kind of healthful dish you've made—and be startled to see how much his friend likes the new food experience!

4. *Give rational reasons* for the dietary changes. Here is where you become not only a parent to your child but also a teacher and even a bit of a salesperson. Here are the most important things your child should understand about why you're making these changes.

- Sugar can make her feel good temporarily, but then cause a letdown that will have her feeling mean and awful (not to mention the effects it will have on her teeth).
- High sugar intake can lead to weight gain and the terrible dis-ease of diabetes.

- Sugar has to be given up entirely because even a little bit is addictive. That's why so many companies fill food with it, you can explain gently, because it "hooks" kids and makes them want to buy more and more.
- Eating continually—especially food with lots of sugar and white flour in it—causes constipation. (Get as gross as you want here. Kids pay attention to gross talk.)
- The human body can use just so many calories in a day. Explain that people who "spend their calories" with fresh, healthful food don't have to worry about getting fat.
- Your new way of eating is also how many of the world's most successful, beautiful, and talented people eat. Actors, athletes, musicians, and others whose careers depend on maintaining their health and energy pay special attention to what they eat.

5. *Show empathy* for your child's reluctance to adopt the new ways of eating. Explain that you know only too well how pleasurable the now-unacceptable food is—how sweet and filling it is and how it makes you feel good when you eat it. You also know how much fun it is to enjoy pizzas and sodas with friends. Explain that you've now come to understand how harmful those foods can be to a child's well-being and how you want your child to feel and look his best—which means eliminating those kinds of foods.

Help him find ways to get around the social pressures so that he can still enjoy those special times with friends—perhaps he can have a smoothie or hard-boiled egg before these gorgings so he won't be hungry. Tell your child how you have fun at luncheons and special occasion dinners without eating unacceptable food. Ask him for ideas about other food occasions.

Let him know you feel pressure from your friends, too, at events like the dessert potluck—during which every contributor's creation must be at least sampled and raved about or you'll be talked about behind your back.

As you discuss these food challenges with your child, together you'll find ways to provide mutual support, and this shared interest will form a stronger bond between you. You'll begin to see that your food changes can bring you and your children closer together. To reiterate: Show empathy for the children's reluctance to change food habits—but implement the changes anyway using the discussion methods just described.

6. *Show genuine care and concern* for animals, plants, persons, and things. This means insisting that the family's foods come from well-cared-for plants on organic farms and from well-nurtured, naturally raised animals on small ranches operating with high standards. It also means demonstrating appreciation for your kitchen and your kitchen utensils—carefully washing all knives, cutting boards, and pans, and making sure you buy the best of these you can afford.

Other ways to show care and concern for your family and the food they eat include serving your food with love on a table that is nicely decorated and set. Make sure the TV is turned off when you eat. Talking about each person's day and about the food as you eat it can bring great calm to your dinnertimes. Show interest in everyone—and don't be afraid to join in some laughter.

Perhaps most of all, showing genuine care for food means not abusing it in quantity. Stop eating when the meal or snack is finished, so your body can properly absorb the nutrients. Food thus becomes a finite experience, to be remembered with joy, rather than just an endless activity. In one of his travel books, Gerald Durrell speaks of a farmer in France whose eyes actually filled with tears of emotion as he described favorite kinds of *fromage*—cheese—he had eaten at various meals. Something that you care about that much, you don't just rush through. You savor and enjoy.

A Last Word about Food and Rudeness

By now, you know that certain foods play a critical role in kids' rudeness and bad attitudes. You also know that forbidding these foods in your home will help a lot. But real changes in rudeness and attitude require more complete changes in your family's food intake; they require you to replace the processed, sugary foods your children were eating with a diet of healthful, whole, fresh foods that are life-sustaining and will make them feel and look great. You can make these changes slowly, or you can choose to make them suddenly, in one fell swoop. If you do resolve to make the changes quickly and your child is indeed suffering from food-induced rudeness, chances are you'll see results in as little as a week.

Whichever kind of change you choose, give yourself a pat on the back. You, by your own informed decision, are taking charge of your family's diet. You are rejecting your well-intentioned but ill-informed relatives. You are stopping the corporate influences of fast-food places, TV advertising, and supermarkets. You are overcoming the negative influences of your kids' friends, their school, and any of the many other modern institutions that say how and what and when your family should eat.

You are making those decisions now. That's showing your family love in one of the best, most nurturing ways of all.

Bon appétit! Good luck!

epilogue

A little bragging music, please.

Now that I've come to the end of this book, I want to tell you that I understand its messages firsthand—as a daughter, sister, granddaughter, and niece, but also, most frighteningly, as a mother. When my son displayed the symptoms so depressingly obvious in other family members—meanness after eating carbs, cravings for sweets, sick fatigue after a fast-food meal, uncontrollable weight gains in adolescence—I took him to several doctors. Most said what my mother did, that he should be able to eat what he wanted and I was overreacting. Didn't I know a little boy needs his treats? Did I want to deprive him of everything?

I then recalled a doctor my mother had consulted when my brother and I were very young and both suffered from asthma. This doctor had diagnosed my brother with hypoglycemia and said he should have protein every few hours. My mother, not able to deprive my brother of anything he wanted, had ignored this doctor's recommended diet. At the age of 13, my brother's weight went up to 300 pounds, and he was diagnosed as an alcoholic after several alcohol-related incidents. (Dr. Cabin recently shed light on this connection for me, describing how alcoholism is actually a physical condition rendering a person unable to metabolize carbohydrates.)

Since that time, my brother's life has been difficult—not just for him, but for everyone who cared about him. My feelings about my brother were, and still are, feelings of loss. A wonderful friend in my childhood, he began slipping away from me in early adolescence and never did come back. I miss him still.

That future was not going to happen to my son, I decided. I forbade him at about the age of 6 to have any sweets or refined carbs, and my husband cooperated. We got him into tennis, a physical activity that was a marvelous outlet all the way into adulthood. Today, my son is slender, good-looking, married to a Southern California beauty, and the father of two incredible daughters, both so enchanting to be with that they take my breath away. I know it sounds mean-spirited to compare my son's life to my brother's. But I do so anyway. I can't help wondering what could have been if my brother had been given the guidance and support he needed concerning his diet and health.

As I've said elsewhere in this book, my brother's story is not unique in my family. Perhaps your family has similar stories. It's so infectious, this food-caused behavior. It can ruin family happiness from one generation to the next.

Does my son appreciate my early efforts on his behalf? Absolutely, positively *not*. He takes his good life completely for granted. That, I've heard, is how it should be if a parent does her job well.

Enough of my bragging. I wish the best lives for your children, too—which is the real reason why I wrote this book.

resources

Natural Foods (Mail-Order Sources)

Diamond Organics

A wide assortment of fresh produce grown organically, shipped right to your door.
PO Box 2159
Freedom, CA 95019
(888) 674-2642
www.diamondorganics.com

Gaiam Inc.

Includes grocery items from Whole Foods Markets available for direct shipment.
360 Interlocken Boulevard, Suite 300
Broomfield, CO 80021-3440
(877) 989-6321
www.gaiam.com

***Organic Style* Magazine**

Product reviews and a comprehensive resource list for organic and natural products.
PO Box 7943
Red Oak, IA 51591
(800) 365-3276
www.organicstyle.com

Vitamins, Minerals, and Supplements (Mail-Order Sources)

Hank and Brian's Vitamins and Minerals
Distributed by Hank and Brian's Adventures in Health
772 North Country Club Drive
Tucson, AZ 85716
(520) 319-0810

Recommended Reading

Nutrition

Prevention magazine. For subscriptions, call (800) 813-8070 or visit www.prevention.com.

Atkins, Robert C. *Dr. Atkins' Age-Defying Diet Revolution*. St. Martin's Press, 1999.

Crook, William G. *The Yeast Connection Handbook*. Professional Books, 1999.

Davis, Adelle. *Let's Have Healthy Children*. Signet, 1981.

Feingold, Ben F. *Why Your Child Is Hyperactive*. Random House, 1975.

Rapp, Doris. *Is This Your Child?: Discovering and Treating Unrecognized Allergies in Children and Adults*. William Morrow and Company, 1992.

Stoddard, Mary Nash. *Deadly Deception: Story of Aspartame*. Odenwald Press, 1998.

Ulene, Art. *The NutriBase Nutrition Facts Desk Reference*. Second edition. Avery Penguin Putnam, 2001.

Healing Foods

Somer, Elizabeth, and Nancy L. Snyderman. *Food and Mood: The Complete Guide to Eating Well and Feeling Your Best.* Second edition. Owl Books, 1999.

Yeager, Selene, and the editors of *Prevention* Health Books. *The Doctors Book of Food Remedies.* Rodale Inc., 1998.

Healthy Cooking

Newman, Bettina, and David Joachim. *Lose Weight the Smart Low-Carb Way: 200 High-Flavor Recipes and a 7-Step Plan to Stay Slim Forever.* Rodale Inc., 2002.

Sahelian, Ray, and Donna Gates. *The Stevia Cookbook: Cooking with Nature's Calorie-Free Sweetener.* Avery Penguin Putnam, 1999.

Organic Gardening

OG. The premier magazine on gardening without chemicals. To order a subscription, call (800) 666-2206 or visit www.organic gardening.com.

Bradley, Fern Marshall, and Barbara W. Ellis, eds. *Rodale's All-New Encyclopedia of Organic Gardening.* Rodale Inc., 1992.

Childrearing

Sneyd, Lynn Wiese. *Holistic Parenting.* McGraw Hill, 2000.

Homemade Crafts for Kids

Editors of *Family Fun* magazine. *Family Fun Crafts: 500 Creative Activities for You and Your Kids.* Hyperion, 1997.

index

Underscored page references indicate sidebars and tables. **Boldface** references indicate illustrations.

C

f

g